Stewart N. Gill

The
Future
of Staff
Groups

The Future of Staff Groups

JOEL P. HENNING

Daring to Distribute Power and Capacity

Berrett-Koehler Publishers, Inc.
San Francisco

Berrett-Koehler Publishers, Inc.
450 Sansome Street, Suite 1200
San Francisco, CA 94111-3320
Tel: (415) 288-0260 Fax: (415) 362-2512

Ordering Information

Individual sales. Berrett-Koehler publications are available through most bookstores. They can also be ordered direct from Berrett-Koehler at the address above.

Quantity sales. Special discounts are available on quantity purchases by corporations, associations, and others. For details, contact the "Special Sales Department" at the Berrett-Koehler address above.

Orders for college textbook/course adoption use. Please contact Berrett-Koehler Publishers at the address above.

Orders by U.S. trade bookstores and wholesalers. Please contact Publishers Group West, 4065 Hollis Street, Box 8843, Emeryville, CA 94662. Tel: (510) 658–3453; 1-800-788-3123. Fax: (510) 658-1834

Printed in the United States of America

 Printed on acid-free and recycled paper that is composed of 50% recovered fiber, including 10% postconsumer waste.

Library of Congress Cataloging-in-Publication Data

Henning, Joel P., 1939–
    The future of staff groups: daring to distribute power and capacity / Joel P. Henning. — 1st ed.
        p.   cm.
    Indluces bibliographical references and index.
    ISBN 1-57675-025-6 (alk. paper)
    1. Personnel management.   I. Title.
HF5549.H4135   1997
658.3—dc21   97-26655
                                                          CIP

First Edition
    00 99 98 97   10 9 8 7 6 5 4 3 2 1

Copyediting: Hilary Powers
Proofreading: PeopleSpeak
Interior design and production: Joel Friedlander Publishing Services
Indexing: Evergreen Valley Indexing
Jacket: Sue Malakowski

TO JIM MASELKO

Who dares to act on faith with hope and optimism

CONTENTS

PREFACE

This book is about the current and future place of staff groups—Human Resources, Finance, Information Systems, and their peers—in large organizations. The future of these staff functions will depend on their direct and explicit contribution to positive business results. The intended audience includes members and managers of staff functions, but the book also speaks to all those who must deal with staff groups as clients or collaborators. The will and desire to write the book is the product of three observations formed and reinforced over two decades of working with staff groups.

Staff groups will have a decisive impact on the future success or failure of a business. The quality of business information, business decisions, new products, and relationships is largely in the hands of staff functions. Yet the power and influence of staff groups to determine success is little recognized. In many ways they are second-class citizens in the corporate community—the bean counters, touchy feely people, computer nerds, or executioners for senior management. Business literature barely takes account of them. Yet it is their expertise, methods, practices, policies, and purposes that often determine the capacity of a business to know, decide, and create. Complaining, berating, blaming, ignoring, or outsourcing are not adequate responses to their influence or importance.

Staff groups and their clients do not know how to successfully talk and work with each other. Both sides are stuck in an antiquated and counterproductive relationship born of a different time and circumstance. Frequently the focus of clients—line managers—is on owning the staff. Control is the point. In their view, a good staff assumes a posture of submission and compliance. Conversations confronting these issues occur on a daily basis, accompanied by frustration, anger, and resignation. It is all for naught. Owning and controlling staff groups is not the point. Pursuing control is irrelevant. The point is understanding how staff groups can and should contribute to business success.

Staff groups, for their part, have their own control issues. They are captivated with attending to senior management and preoccupied with managing relationships. They are the eyes and ears of senior management, hoping to create value by becoming an extension of senior management's will—as they project it. Or they spend endless hours deliberating and strategizing about how to get senior management to "sign up for" or "buy in to" what they want to do. Positioning and packaging are everything. They rejoice when their programs are sponsored and mandated by those in power. They hold their clients hostage by denying them choice. They fear their clients will seek revenge if ever they are given choice about where to acquire staff expertise. This preoccupation with sponsorship, mandates, sole sourcing, and relationships is all misplaced energy. It is extraneous. It distracts staff from focusing on the only really important question: How does it contribute to building the capacity of the business to survive and prosper in the marketplace?

With clients intent on control and staff groups preoccupied with upward-serving activity, it is no wonder that their conversations and work together are mutually disappointing.

Both clients and staff must change if the full measure of the staff's contribution to the business is to be realized. For clients it means abandoning their preoccupation with control and the assumption that they know best how to employ the expertise staff brings. It means taking seriously the staff's own viewpoint about how it can contribute to the business. It means demanding staff be relevant to the business and willing to offer promises and guarantees about its business impact.

For staff it means forsaking the fixation with its relationship to senior management. It means becoming clear, concise, and compelling about how staff expertise can build the capacity of the business it serves. It means choosing accountability for creating a *staff business* that offers something of worth. It means putting everything at risk by offering promises and guarantees about business impact.

It is not what we do notice or pay attention to that does us in; it is what we don't see or pay attention to that harms us. For organizations to ignore or pay scant attention to staff groups is to put themselves in peril. Knowing, deciding, relating, and creating are the lifeblood of a successful enterprise. How these things are done is the work of staff groups.

How they are done will lead to success or failure. It is my hope that this book offers a viable and promising road to building the capacity of staff groups to make the fullest possible contribution to the institutions they serve.

—Joel P. Henning
Rupert, Vermont
August, 1997

Acknowledgments

I suspect until people undertake writing a book they are not fully aware that the acknowledgment of others' contributions is so profoundly important. What I write here is done with deep humility and appreciation.

Without Jim Maselko and Louis Savary this book would never have been. They believed I could write long before I had any faith.

Hilary Powers taught me about good will, clarity, and gentle persuasion in editing this book. She brought to the task a deep understanding of the subject matter, the mind of the reader, and the heart of an author. She is superbly suited to do her work and I have been honored by her service.

Berrett-Koehler is the publisher of this book and a very special group of people. Each person I have met brings heart, mind, and hands to their work. They care deeply about who they are and what they do in the world—and what they do they do superbly.

James Showkeir and Derek Millard labor to apply these ideas every day in their consulting work. They have been friends, colleagues, and unselfish contributors. Their fingerprints are on every page.

Pat Mucci has the patience of Job and the persistence of Sisyphus. She has been a gift to me.

Throughout the writing of this book, Jayne Sanford has been my lifeline to the world. She has made a thousand calls, anticipated what I needed, and supported me through the frustration and dark moments of this venture. I owe her flowers.

Everyone at Designed Learning—including Kayleen Kane, Jerry Pavloff, Phil Grosnick, Janet Newell, and those already mentioned—has earned my affection and respect for his or her support and good will. But far more important, these people have been my brothers and sisters in creating and living out in our life together the ideas contained in this book.

To all those who have read this book and offered gentle and insightful feedback, I offer my thanks.

ACCOUNTABILITY FOR SERVICE AND CHANGE

This is a book about personal and organizational choices in the face of jarring realities. Staff groups live in an uneasy and difficult world. There is increased demand they demonstrate relevance and contribution to business results. There is persistent and gnawing doubt about the content of their contribution. The changes required of staff groups to respond successfully to all this are not packaging and positioning issues. The answer, in most cases, is not to try harder at what they have been doing. The answer, in part, requires a rebuilding of their foundations: how they define themselves, on what basis they claim legitimacy, what they pay attention to, what they offer to their clients.

Even doing all this is not enough. At the heart of the changes required are personal choices for accountability. If we fail to confront this issue, no change will be fully successful. Are we each willing to embrace risk and danger, and forsake safety and comfort? In the end, all change is personal. Because I am so firmly convinced of the necessity of embracing the personal changes presented in this book, I begin with two stories about my own struggles with change and accountability.

ON THE HOME FRONT

A number of years ago, I separated from my wife, Judy. The specific reasons for the separation are not important. They were the ordinary ones, born of dissatisfaction with unmet wishes. I wanted her to be responsible for making me feel appreciated, loved, sexy, safe, important, and strong. I believed if I could find ways to please her she would become the lover and wife I wanted her to be. I said yes when I meant no and no when I wanted to say yes. I went to the ballet, learned to play tennis, and even took up jogging—things Judy loved—in hopes that pleasing her would get me what I wanted. I held my tongue when irritated and feigned enthusiastic interest in meditation and yoga. I read books, dutifully went to therapy, and deliberated with friends in hopes of finding a way to make Judy into who I wanted her to be. I did it all. I bartered with her for my happiness and she bartered with me. In the end there was disappointment and bitterness for both of us.

Six months into the separation, Judy and I met for dinner. The purpose of our meeting was to discuss reconciliation. After some small talk, Judy got to the point and stated her wish that we reconcile. She went on to state simply and briefly that she would embrace a reconciliation with faith and what she called "persistence." She had only two requests of me. One was that I would choose to be optimistic about our marriage and its future; the other, that I choose commitment to the success of the marriage. "I am offering you optimism and commitment. There is nothing else I want from you," she said, "but these are essentials—that both you and I bring optimism and commitment to any reconciliation."

My response had the tone of "I think we can make a deal." What I actually said to her was, "Well, I understand that you want optimism and commitment from me, and I think I can deliver those. There are only a few things I want from you." I went on to enumerate the changes I wanted to see in her—things that would please me or remedy some past disappointment.

In hindsight, I can see how trivial and laughable they were, but at the time I was quite serious. I wanted Judy to demonstrate "more appreciation for the considerable effort I make to provide a high standard of living for this family." I wanted her to acknowledge "the difficulty of the sacrifices I make month after month, being away from home, on the road every week, living out of a suitcase," and so on. I also had a number of wishes about how her time and attention were to be directed on the few occasions when I was home. For instance, when I returned from a business trip, I expected "to see the house in order." I did not want to be "met at the door by a mob of our children's friends." While I was at home, I wanted family time directed to accommodate me, and "to do what I want to do."

I felt generous in not having a long list of conditions for reconciliation. In conclusion, I said to her, "And if you're willing to make these changes, then I'm willing to come back into the marriage with optimism and commitment."

After I finished talking, I thought there would be reason for celebration—that we had struck an agreeable bargain. Wrong! Judy became quite serious. "Joel, I feel sad," she said. "If that's the deal you want to make, I don't think it will work, and I think a divorce is inevitable."

At that moment, I was confused, shocked, and irritated. I thought I had come a long way in being accommodating to her. It sounded as if she hadn't even heard me.

I said to her, "What's the problem? I said yes to your requests and it doesn't seem that my requests are all that difficult to deliver on. What's the big deal?"

Her reply was, "Joel, you are willing to choose for optimism and commitment *only if I make some changes*. You want *me* to be accountable for *your* happiness and commitment. The moment I don't show enough appreciation you're going to say to me, 'Judy, you didn't do your part. I'm withdrawing my commitment.'"

She added, "That's not the deal I want, Joel. I want you to choose for optimism and commitment without bartering with me. If I'm the one who has to create the circumstances to sustain your optimism and commitment, then I'm the one who is *responsible* for your optimism and commitment. That's exactly what the deal has been between us for the last ten years. We've tried that; it hasn't worked. I will not do the same thing all over again."

I didn't get it. I saw life and relationships as a process of barter. I did not understand what she meant, and it would be some time before I would.

In my bargaining with Judy, I had wanted to hold her accountable for my optimism and commitment, based on her meeting the conditions I set. What she was asking of me was revolutionary. She was asking me to choose for accountability, optimism, and commitment on my own—without barter. She wanted to know if optimism for the marriage was a commitment I would choose to make independent of her actions.

I still wanted to focus the conversation on the ways that Judy could please me and end the pain. I held her accountable for my comfort and despair, my joy and frustration. I believed these were all in her hands. They were hers to give or withhold. I had little or no interest in discussing or considering unbartered commitment and optimism. Everything depended on what she did and how she felt. She held the keys to the survival of the marriage and my emotional well-being. I was bound to focus my attention on her. If she would not change, I conjectured, there was somebody out there who would never disappoint me, always take me seriously, treat me fairly, and create the world in which I wanted to live.

In essence, she told me, "We can be absolutely certain that at some point we will surely let each other down; we will have moments when we think we've been unfairly treated. Those are inescapable parts of any long-term relationship. What's important in sustaining the relationship, in the face of inevitable disappointment, is to continue choosing for faith and tenacity."

"I am no different from you," she said. "I live in a world of disappointments too. I live in a world where I see injustice. Some of the time you disappoint me. Some of the time you are unfair or lack compassion." She added, "Don't you get it, Joel? There is enough disappointment in the world for all of us to despair and enough injury in the world to make cynics of us all. My God, the evidence is endless, and it will be endless until the day we die. The only thing we control, the only thing that makes a difference in the face of all this, is the response I choose and the response you choose. What position do you choose to take in the world? Do you surrender to the disappointments and the injustices in life? Do you choose to become the cynic? Do you choose helplessness? Do you choose to become a bystander in the face of it all? Or do you say, 'Yes, that's what the world is. In the face of that jarring reality, I choose for optimism. I choose for commitment, I choose for accountability. I'll deal with the disappointment and injustice as best I can.' Who I want to be in this world is not someone who ends up bitter, angry, and helpless. Even in very difficult circumstances, my intention is to act with enthusiasm and persistence. What I know, Joel, is that in the end it is futile to focus my attention on you or the world. The really important conversations are not about how you should please me or how you have disappointed me. The only important conversation is about what I want to offer, who I choose to be in this relationship. Period."

The thought of choosing accountability for my own commitment and optimism in the relationship struck terror in my heart. "Anybody but me, Lord!" Yet it was clear to me the only hope for the survival of our relationship was in making that choice.

This book is not about marriage. It is not about my relationship with Judy. It is about the lessons I learned from my conversations with her as they apply to the workplace.

What are the connections to the workplace, to serving others, and to the survival and prosperity of a business? What would it mean to choose accountability for my work without conditions, without barter?

REPETITION AS A USEFUL MEANS OF LEARNING

Not long after my conversation with Judy I had the good fortune to learn the same lesson all over again. I was working at a major corporation in San Francisco. It was one of my very first long-term consulting contracts. I had opportunities I had never had before. I had access to senior managers. I was being taken seriously. I was feeling successful and important.

Life was good.

One afternoon, late in the day, I got a call from the administrative assistant to the CEO, Jim. She inquired about my immediate availability, "Jim wants to see you as soon as possible. Could you come over right away?" Could I come over right away? Earthquake and fire could not have stopped me. Jim wanted to see me—immediately—I was about to enter into the big time. If only my mother were alive to see how it all turned out.

I was ushered into Jim's office. It was unlike any office I had ever seen. The windows looked out at a panoramic view of the Golden Gate Bridge. Everything was done in white with the exception of a green cactus and Jim's highly polished black walnut desk, which was positioned catty-cornered facing the Bay view. Jim sat behind it and behind Jim an alcove was cut into the wall and backlit. The effect was to create an aura that surrounded Jim. I was impressed.

Greetings were exchanged. I sat down to listen, prepared to be as helpful as possible. Jim began, "Jack, I appreciate your coming so soon. I've got a problem and I think you can help solve it." I made no attempt to remind Jim that my name was Joel. I could live with Jack, at least for the time being. Why interrupt a conversation that was going so well?

He continued, "You have been working with Bob over the last few months. He thinks highly of you. You clearly have some influence with him. I believe it is time for Bob to give up the leadership of the International Division and take a staff job in Corporate Planning. I have discussed this with him several times. He is very resistant to the move, doesn't think he is suited to a staff position. If you were to advise him to make the move I think he would do it. What I have in mind is for you to talk to him and get this thing settled."

There was a long and acrimonious history between Bob and Jim. I suspected that this move was the beginning of the end for Bob. I also knew that intervening in the manner that Jim desired was at best a poor use of my expertise. I responded, "Jim, it seems to me that it would be better if you dealt with Bob directly about the move and any difficult issues that may surround it. If it would be helpful, I would be glad to sit in on the conversation."

The moment of death is not the only time your life passes before your eyes. Jim paused for a moment and then quietly commented, "I don't find that remark at all helpful, Jack." If there has ever been a moment in my life when I was convinced that my survival on every level was in the hands of others, this was it. I was about to lose my most important consulting contract. Months and years of work were in the balance. The financial consequences would be very difficult. All the positioning I had worked so hard to achieve would be lost. If I was going to survive I had to do something and I had to do it now. I leaned forward, looked Jim in the eye and said, "Now I understand what you want. I'll talk to Bob this afternoon." The meeting ended. I left the office.

The end of the story is not important. I met with Bob and told him what had happened; he could do what he wished with the information. The important part of the story is what happened in my heart and mind in the moments after I left the meeting with Jim. I would have predicted that I would be angry with myself for surrendering, for saying yes when I meant no. But I wasn't mad at myself, I was mad at Jim. He had compromised me. He had manipulated me. He had threatened me. He . . . he . . . he. . . .

In the end, accommodation gained nothing. Jim never talked with me again. I was asked to leave the organization within months of my meeting with Jim. Upon reflection I believe

Jim knew that I had failed him. I said yes when I meant no. I chose concession over contribution.

LESSONS LEARNED FROM JUDY AND JIM

Marriage is marriage. Work is work. They are different in countless respects. However, I bring myself to both of them: my viewpoint, my ways of understanding, my notions of how things work. *With both Judy and Jim I was convinced, even certain, that my survival and success were in their hands.* It was their choices that would control my safety, security, emotional well-being, and identity in the world. Convinced of this, it is no wonder that paying attention to what they said, did, and felt was an imperative priority. With each of them the relationship became a barter. Pleasing them was the tactic; disappointment, the outcome.

I did not understand that new purposes cannot be embraced and authentic change pursued so long as attention is primarily focused on others' reactions as opposed to my intentions.

JUDY, JIM, AND THE WORLD OF STAFF

The staff world is troubled and unsettled. The time when safety and career tracks were predictable and certain has passed. Old formulas for success and survival no longer work. Staff groups find themselves caught in cycles of trying to please those they serve followed by discouragement and frustration with the response they get.

They continue to be preoccupied with paying attention to upward-serving relationships, believing their survival depends on the approval and blessing of those who hold power. Endless hours are spent in anticipation of contact with senior managers. Conversations are crafted, the right presenter recruited, state-of-the-art overheads produced, and timing decided. The only important question at the end of the day is "How did it go?" It is code for "Did we *please* them?" Beneath it all is an attempt to barter. If we can please we will succeed and survive. Paying attention to the relationship is everything!

All too often, attempts to secure future safety through pleasing someone end in failure. Frustration and discouragement are common. Conversations outlining the failures of senior management to appreciate staff are frequent and heated.

No one is sure how to navigate in these circumstances. If loyalty and being a willing pair of hands are no longer sufficient for a place at the table, what is the path? Trying harder at pleasing is not the answer.

Judy's point was "Joel, it is not about what I do, it is about who you want to be and what you want to offer. It is about you. Period." For staff groups it means forsaking their upward-serving preoccupation with pleasing and their wish to win a place at the table by elegant packaging. It means turning their attention on themselves. It means risking their survival on the content of their contribution. It means choosing accountability for their survival and success without barter or conditions.

The Choice for Accountability

When I am at work, I have choices. I can choose—as an act of will and courage—to be accountable for being the very best I can be. I can choose to be accountable to carry into work optimism about what is possible. I can choose to take my work seriously, to put myself on the line about serving others and having an impact on the business. I can choose commitment for that impact and hold myself accountable for achieving it.

Or I can find a hundred ways to avoid the choice. I can construct endless excuses about why it's not my fault or why things are the way they are.

As I desperately wanted to avoid personal accountability for my marriage, so, too, did I want to avoid personal accountability to a client. I discovered the lessons I learned from Judy applied to more than my marriage; those lessons would have a profound impact on my relationship to clients and work.

A Note About Method

I have selected several primary cases to illustrate and give life to the ideas presented in the book. Some readers have noted that the recurring stories give the impression of a very small sample for some very large conclusions. "Maybe more examples would help the credibility of your thesis," the gently delivered suggestion runs. In my defense I believe that the changes discussed are better understood in the context of a movie than a photograph. I've found that the transformation described here does not occur as a sudden outcome of an epiphanal experience; it is more the result of a rather difficult and arduous trek. The challenge is

r of finding the will to skydive for the first time; it is more
the will to hike the Appalachian Trail. Sound bites and
cameo stories don't make the point well. Therefore I persist in returning
to the same cases as the book progresses.

In Conclusion

The change I am talking about in this book had to be lived out, both in
my marriage and in my work. I had to grasp that the road to my salva-
tion involved *choosing* to live in a difficult world where there would be
defeats, where there is no safe place. It demanded choosing to be in that
world with a deep wish and intention to have an impact, and to do it
with energy, tenacity, and good will. Taking that stance was and is now
fundamental to the survival of my soul. The chapters that follow repeatedly confront these issues.

Most of us have to get up and go to work every day. Furthermore, most
of us don't have the luxury of going to workplaces where people understand everything we say, take us seriously all the time, and never disappoint us. Instead, we experience frustration, don't feel we're taken
seriously, and wonder how we're ever going to have any impact. The temptation is to surrender. The temptation is very strong. It is easy to succumb.

This book is about an alternative path, the path of unconditional
commitment and accountability to service and work. It requires the
transformation of the individual and traditional notions of service. It may
be the only path for the survival and success of the staff professions.

Faced with a global economy that is more and more demanding, it
is imperative that each of us take the alternative path if we're going to
contribute and create work in which we can believe. Making an
unbartered choice for commitment to the success of our colleagues and
clients is becoming less of an option. It's being forced on us by the jarring realities of the marketplace. We can embrace the choice—or spend
our time, at any price, trying to avoid its demand.

What the world of work needs is not more management techniques
and programs. What it needs is a fundamental redefinition of each person's commitment to the success of the organization and to their participation in the workplace. All of us face choices that will profoundly affect
ourselves and our work.

INTENTION AND THEORY

Part I lays out the background, describing how and why the proposed approach to staff groups serves both clients and staff better than the old one. It treats the change required of staff groups as one that starts with defining themselves as businesses at risk. They need to see the difference between customers and bankers, and to accept that customers have choice about where they get services and that bankers have a right to expect a return on their investment. Progress begins when a staff group insists on accountability for its business impact.

Chapter One explores these factors in detail, outlining the difficult future staff groups now face. Chapter Two proposes the first steps in redefining the staff role. It discusses what staff groups invite by defining themselves as businesses at risk—forsaking protection and caution, betting survival and success on performance in the marketplace, and needing to create more value than cost in the eyes of the consumer. A group that risks its future on the free choice of its customers will soon find out what good services and products entail.

After Chapter Two is the first "Practical Interlude"—a list of specific questions that will help a staff group define itself as a business at risk. Part II will contain several more such interludes, all designed to make the material easier to grasp and use in real life.

Chapter Three addresses the next step, making an offer—that is, choosing to translate technology into an offer to the clients that will build their competence to survive and prosper. The offer must be so focused on substance that it puts a staff group at risk. It requires making a promise, providing a guarantee, and choosing consequences for not fulfilling the promise. Chapter Four goes on to discuss staff competence and expertise. It explores the difficulty of jettisoning old products and creating new ones in service to the client.

Chapter Five points out that the theory and its practice need not be grim—indeed, they require hope, optimism, and good will. The process is not easy and it is not safe, but it can be joyful. If you make it work for you, it will allow you to take your heart to the office along with your head and your wallet.

The following chart summarizes the key learning points of the theory presented in Part I:

REDEFINING THE STAFF OUTLOOK
Choose to be a business at risk.
Make senior management the banker.
Make core work units the customers.
Change conversations with customers and senior management.
Give customers choice.

REORIENTING STAFF ACTIVITY
Lay claim to an expertise.
Connect the use of expertise to business results.
Construct a compelling business argument for using it.
Insist on promises and guarantees based on results.
Advocate for client choice.

MAKING A DIFFERENCE
Identify the core competence.
Choose a stance about the use of expertise.
Create the business argument to support the stance.
Develop relevant products and services.

CHAPTER 1

THE JARRING REALITY

Striking a balance is hard. The issues this book attempts to define and address are about the world and at the same time personal. Notions like the global marketplace, large multinational corporations, and complex technologies emphasize how finite any one of us is. What is the significance of any one person's experience in the face of these realities? Yet each one of us must in some way respond to these forces. It is in the response we make to them that they and we can be changed and transformed. Institutions don't change until you and I change. We are inescapably tied together. In the end all change is personal and happens one person at a time. To talk of the business world without paying attention to the personal makes no sense.

FROM JUDY TO THE WORLD

To succeed at change, I must understand the world and myself. If I do not understand myself I am a loose cannon. If I do not understand the world, I will defeat my own efforts to change and influence it, or at best, success will be an accident. I talk of Judy and Jim because they have taught me to understand myself and how I am tempted to respond to all that goes on around me. I discuss the world—corporations, staff groups, technologies—because it is the arena in which I live and work. It is my intent to pay attention to both throughout this book and to make clear the powerful connection between them.

DEFINING TERMS AND A STANCE

Throughout this book, I use a number of terms that may have different meanings to different readers. Therefore, it may be useful to let you know in advance the definitions I attach to them.

Staff and *staff groups* in this book are Human Resources, Finance, Quality, Information Systems, and their peer functions in large organizations. In theory, staff groups share two things. One, their clients are primarily other departments in their organization such as Sales, Distribution, and Manufacturing. Two, staff groups each lay claim to a specialized expertise that is too complex or changes too rapidly to be easily mastered by others. Maintaining the quality and depth of the expertise requires that it be housed in a specialized unit.

Expertise, technology, and *competence* are used interchangeably throughout the book. They refer to the theories and methods mastered by staff groups and offered to their clients with the promise of improving business results. Finance has theories and methods that create useful financial measures for clients. Among other things, Information Systems lays claim to theories and methods that allow information to be retrieved, manipulated, and distributed in ways that inform and create business intelligence. Human Resources has theories and methods to effectively organize collective effort in customer organizations. It is this expertise, competence, and technology that make staff groups potentially valuable to clients.

Capacity refers to the potential a business has to improve its profitability, the quality of its products, its cycle times, and its positioning in the marketplace. Maximum capacity is achieved when a business can bring to bear on every task its best collective intelligence, clearest intentions, and most effective and efficient action. The most important function of staff groups is to build the capacity of client organizations. This is the end the application of their expertise should serve.

A *stance* is the position a staff group takes about the proper intention and use of its technology within client organizations. It is the stance of this book that staff groups most effectively build capacity in a client organization by using their expertise to distribute power widely rather than to centralize it.

The *components of power* in organizations are literacy about the business, choice, access to resources, competence, and accountability. When all these are present in an action, effective power is exercised. Maximum capacity is realized in a business unit when every member is literate about the business, is empowered to make choices and access resources in service of the business, possesses the competence to take effective action, and chooses personal accountability for service to the business. If these components of power are thinly distributed, the capacity of the organization to focus intelligence, intention, and effective action is seriously limited. If the components of power are broadly distributed, its capacity to focus is greatly enhanced.

Staff groups possess profound power in organizations, although it is generally unacknowledged and invisible. They frequently control and always influence how literacy is distributed, who has the right to make choices and access resources, where accountability is assigned, and how competence is distributed.

Of course, other stances about the use of staff expertise are legitimate. Traditionally, staff expertise has been used to consolidate and centralize literacy, choice, access to resources, competence, and accountability. Many would argue that this is still the role of staff groups. It is a valid point of view—but not the viewpoint of this book. The relevance of this book does not depend on the stance a staff group takes. Nonetheless, throughout this book I will argue for the stance I have chosen: thus the title, *The Future of Staff Groups: Daring to Distribute Power and Capacity.*

A *unique response* to the customer is a response that addresses each customer's specific needs. A mass, take-it-or-leave-it approach to service tends to be self-defeating when customers can easily turn to alternative suppliers. Few companies have captive customers in this age of global markets, just as few staff groups can count on permanent ties to their companies' line units, so it is necessary to strive for a unique response at every level.

THE SURVIVAL OF STAFF GROUPS

There is no place left to hide. Every unit within an organization and every person within a unit is at risk. No one is exempt. All employees are being questioned about the value they bring to the survival and growth of their organization. Any hope to survive simply based on showing up, doing what you are told, and being loyal to the company stands on shaky ground.

We live in a marketplace without boundaries, where many providers compete for every dollar and every customer. Somewhere, someone is thinking about how to make a better offer to your customers than you do.

Organizations can no longer afford the cost of guaranteeing the security of their people. They can't afford the cost of carrying people who are not accountable for business results. Nowhere is the harsh reality of that trend becoming more evident than in staff groups in large organizations.

A Finance person recently confessed to me, "All the assumptions I made about my security and financial safety have collapsed. The world is changing all around me, and I don't feel that I can escape any longer. What can I do in the face of it? What will happen when people seriously question what I do? What if they find it lacking, don't find value in it, and don't want to pay for it anymore?"

I asked him about his worst fear.

"What's my worst fear?" He was silent, then came a moment of realization. "My worst fear is that my customers will be given a choice and that they won't choose me or my staff. Whether they do it out of revenge for our past intrusions or because they see us as irrelevant does not matter. A 'No' would mean that my staff and I have been judged a waste of money and have brought no value to the business.

"In the worst case they would say, 'You were worse than a waste of money because you interfered in our lives with your mandates and endless procedural requirements. We simply wanted to get on with the work. All the red tape you put us through when we wanted to modify a procedure—we couldn't because Finance—you—said no. We no longer have to suffer fools gladly.' That's my worst fear."

STAFF GROUPS: A PROTECTED SPECIES

For a very long time, staff groups in organizations—Finance, Engineering, Information Systems, Human Resources, and Quality—have enjoyed protection from the reality of competition. Some peculiar attitudes result from this protected position.

A GLIMPSE OF REALITY

The setting is the third day of a three-day training session for a business unit at a large insurance company. It's early morning. The external trainer, Carolyn, arrives and speaks to the internal Human Resources coordinator. "I received a lot of feedback from the participants yesterday that this workshop had no relevance to their work. I think we need to raise the issue with the group and let them decide if they want to proceed." Face in a grimace, the internal Human Resources coordinator leans across his desk and says, "I don't give a damn whether they like it or not. You are going to go in there and you are going to conduct this program just as it says in the design."

This coordinator did not feel the hazard of being a business at risk. He felt protected, entitled, and free to ignore the customer. We adopt such attitudes at our own peril.

LIVING AT RISK

It's not that someone in a high place decreed that it would be a good thing to put people and groups at risk. The marketplace wills it.

No longer are staff people in organizations free to ignore the impact they have—or don't have—on the business they serve. Their business impact on profitability, quality, cycle time, or marketplace positioning is quickly becoming a survival issue. They are and will continue to be what counts. Staff groups are having to confront issues that call into question what they do, what they know, and how they bring value.

Nowhere is this more evident than in Human Resources. Too often HR staff has been presenting the same programs over and over again— succession planning, management training, and attitude surveys. For decades, organizational development groups within Human Resources have been developing communication skills, facilitating meetings, and building teams. Human Resources groups within most organizations have also had substantial responsibilities for managing transactions and ensuring policy alignment throughout the organization. They are expected to be the authorities on the company policy manual and to monitor its application throughout the organization.

As organizations examine every dollar of expense, these traditional and long-accepted Human Resources practices are being questioned. What value does traditional Human Resources activity bring to the bottom line of this organization? How do Human Resources programs improve the quality of our service to customers? How does their technology shorten our cycle time or allow us to give a unique response in the marketplace? Really, what is the point of what they do?

It is a struggle to connect traditional activities directly with the desired business outcomes. This is the heart of the problem. There is honest doubt that any credible argument connects the two.

REALITY STRIKES AGAIN

The experience of a manufacturing plant in Southwest Texas, struggling for survival, makes the point. The plant manager knows that five miles away across the Rio Grande is a Mexican plant that can get a garment out the door at far less cost than he can. "Every day we are struggling to lower our unit cost so the six hundred people employed here will have jobs. Who arrives at our doorstep but Human Resources with a mandated program from corporate headquarters about values training. They will force us to carve two days out of every operator's life to go through this stuff. The result will be increased unit costs. During those two days, we are not going to get out any product. Why must I take everybody to a two-day mandated program in the light of what we are facing? I don't need a program about values, I want something that can help us lower unit cost. If I say no, I will pay the price. For those of us out in the world trying to survive, this is nonsense!"

Finance groups have the same difficulty connecting their traditional activities with hard business outcomes. Traditionally, Finance groups have had responsibility for overseeing the annual budget-building process, conducting strategic planning sessions with senior management, assuring compliance with financial procedures, aggregating numbers, and creating reports for the edification of senior management. Finance staffs are facing questions like these: How do these traditional activities bring value to the business or improve the bottom line of this organization? How do all these reports to senior management ensure increased profitability or more satisfied customers?

Information Systems has not escaped doubts and questions. For some Information Systems groups, preoccupation with controlling the kinds of hardware and software that their clients use has become their central mission. Can such control activities offer a reason for being, a reason to claim legitimate membership in the organization? They face questions like these: Does the investment in Information Systems bring value to this company? Are our products better? Are we faster? Are we more profitable? Is our market share growing as a result of the activity of our Information Services function?

At best, there are doubts; at worst, the answer is no. Frequently the doubts and reservations of the organization take the form of *outsourcing*—a rapidly growing phenomenon.

A foreign auto manufacturer operating in the United States recently decided that staff services were going to be cut in the face of financial and marketplace pressures. It began by outsourcing 100 percent of the Information Systems group as well as 80 percent of the Human Resources group. As management looked at each of the remaining staff groups, the choice was either to eliminate the function altogether or to outsource it. Just like that!

A very large computer manufacturer, forced to reduce costs, outsourced a substantial amount of its Finance function on the grounds that the in-house group was too expensive. When a better offer came in from the outside, management took it. Just like that!

At a premier pharmaceutical company, the entire Benefits Department was outsourced to an independent contractor because the contractor could process transactions at less cost with higher quality.

In large organizations, many Organizational Development groups that haven't been outsourced have been eliminated because no one could make a credible argument for the value they bring. Reciting long lists of activities and programs is an unconvincing argument.

None of this is news.

We no longer live in a world where our work, and its direct connection to critical business outcomes, will escape examination. If staff groups are not worried, it's because they are asleep or in a state of denial.

CLIENTS ARE REBELLING

The starting place is to come to terms with the evidence. For years, as a staff person, I enjoyed a comfortable and secure life. I performed services I was familiar with and got paid well. I enjoyed a privileged position.

Today, all that has changed. My position and my comfort are now threatened. Clients now question the value of activities I have been doing for years. They want me to demonstrate the value I bring to what their organizations care deeply about—business results! They want me to show that what I do will make a difference. Questions are being asked that I never had to answer before.

My experience is not unique. Organizations—from executives to core work units—are taking a harder look not only at Human Resources but at Finance, Engineering, Information Systems, and Quality and asking just what value these staff groups bring to the organization. Other staff groups have similar experiences.

Engineering Staff. In a manufacturing plant, industrial engineers working with the operators insist on specific work procedures rather than permitting the operators to create a work process that would successfully deal with new and rapidly changing production demands. The engineers are interfering directly with the operators' ability to respond to the marketplace quickly and effectively—and asking to be paid for it.

Information Systems Staff. An engineer responsible for the redesign of an automobile tells Information Systems, "You won't allow us to use software that will let us create the designs we envision. I have to wait for you—the Systems group—to maybe someday, somewhere, somehow, provide an adaptation of your in-house software to do a small piece of what I could do today with software I could get from an outside vendor. You make us crazy because you prevent us from being able to get the job done!"

It happened at a major U.S. auto maker.

THE CAD/CAM CASE STUDY

The CAD/CAM department, an Information Systems staff group,

was fundamental to the success of the company's design and engineering function. CAD/CAM saw as central to its mission the exclusion of outside software vendors, even when their products were superior and could be adapted to the internal system. The designers and engineers were well aware that better software was available than they could get from the CAD/CAM group. They were utterly frustrated by their inability to get approval from CAD/CAM to buy it. It did not occur to the CAD/CAM group that providing the best possible software for these engineers and designers was fundamental to its own survival.

It was inevitable that CAD/CAM's clients, the designers and engineers, would ask, "Why are we paying these people who are keeping us from making a superior product? They won't allow us to get the software support we need when it is readily available."

Finance Staff. Finance staff groups often assume they have a standing invitation to go where they please in an organization and ask whatever questions occur to them. They serve senior management directly, so their needs take precedence over merely local priorities—sometimes up to and including getting the product out the door.

THE INSURANCE FINANCE CASE STUDY
In a national insurance company a team of twenty or thirty had responsibility for four or five large corporate clients. Each client wanted major exceptions to the company's standard policy. In essence each client wanted a unique response. The company's medical insurance units, responsible for crafting these unique responses, were always asking themselves, "Will we still be profitable if we give this exception? Can we give this exception here without giving it there?"

Frequently, while these insurance units were in the midst of working to accommodate clients, the Finance group would arrive demanding immediate retrieval of data so it could construct upward-bound reports. These reports had no practical relevance to the work teams. Finance's demands took hours away from productive work. They required searching through filing cabinets and running computer programs. Even though the data had no relevance to the work of these highly pressured medical insurance teams, the Finance staff felt entitled to walk in and make the demand. If anybody had given it a hard time, the Finance staff would have found the means to ensure compliance.

This is an intolerable situation in a marketplace where the customer is in charge and there is little forgiveness.

THE DEMAND FOR CHOICE

If line units don't shout it out loud in the middle of these painful situations with staff groups, they shout it silently: "It's not just that we have to bear the cost of you people in staff positions, we have to endure your interference in our business for reasons that make no sense to us. And if the things you get paid to do ever had value, that day has long since passed. We are stopped from being as competitive as we could be by your endless intrusions. We will not live with it! The business can no longer live with it! And the marketplace will not tolerate it!" If staff groups fear that line groups given a choice will seek revenge, they simply show a sane understanding of the problem.

People in line units are demanding choice. And at many companies they are going to get choice because top management is bright enough to see the point. "We can't let staff groups keep our organization from creating the kind of products and services the customer demands."

Eventually, the industrial engineers in the Texas plant are not only going to be outsourced, they are going to be eliminated. Short of a few ergonomic concerns that can be met in other ways, if industrial engineers are getting in the way of production, what's the point of having them?

Claiming legitimacy because we audit, oversee, and ensure alignment is a balloon about to burst. Organizations simply can't afford to pay people to watch as a full-time job. They can't afford people who see their only task as to control and audit core work groups.

Claiming legitimacy because we show up and do programs that we have been doing for years is not enough. If we do not have a credible and compelling business case for the worth of our program, it will not endure.

You may say that line units are being resistant. You can call it resistance or label it whatever you want. If you do, you miss the point. The fundamental issue is that people in organizations are looking staff groups in the eye and asking, "What do you bring to our unit that lets us reduce our unit cost, design a better product, or deal more uniquely with customers? Tell us how your service builds our capacity to do any of that. We don't see it."

THE FUTURE OF STAFF GROUPS

If you add all this up, what's the point? Clearly, from the viewpoint of line units—those who are supposed to be the clients of the staff groups—traditional staff services are not working. A day of reckoning is fast approaching. "You are costing us money. You are not helping. Worse yet, you are interfering directly with our ability to carry on our business in a way that is responsive to the client. We're not going to stand for it anymore. When our survival is at stake, why should we continue to tolerate your cost and interference in our life?"

What does all this mean? Where does this path of reasoning take staff groups? Is outsourcing the future of all staff groups?

The answers depend on how staff groups respond to the reality facing them. If they continue to audit, oversee, and force mandated programs and practices on line groups, the outcome is predictable. The marketplace will rule. Staff groups that burden line units with slow, bureaucratic, inward-looking procedures and processes are going to die.

Is there another option for staff groups besides elimination or business failure? The only alternative I know of is for staff groups to face the difficult issue head on and get clear about what changes are required if they are going to survive and contribute to the business they are supposed to serve.

IN CONCLUSION

You will remember there came a critical moment in my marriage to Judy when I had to face the painful truth that my marriage was not working, and that something quite different was required of me. I could either look straight at what I had to face and deal with it, or I could deny it.

It is no different for staff groups. The day when you and I can claim entitlement is over. The day when you and I can claim privilege is over. The day when you and I are excused from accountability for business outcomes is over.

You and I may hope that we can last doing what we have always done. Or we can face the same issue I had to face at dinner with Judy and across the desk from Jim.

The question is, "Am I willing to risk the future on the content of my contribution? Am I willing to embrace and demand of myself responsibility for having an impact on results? Am I willing to do all of this with optimism and good will?"

If you make that choice and are willing to take that stand, it will change everything you do in your staff work.

This choice is not about working harder at what you have always been doing. It is not about fixing a strained relationship with your clients by being more therapeutic. This choice is about standing in a place you have never stood before, looking at your organization in a way you never looked at it before, and putting yourself on the line in a way you have never been on the line before.

We each have the choice.

Such a choice demands that we redefine our place and purpose.

We must, first of all, figure out whether we can create value in our organization, because if we can't, the right decision is to leave.

With Judy, I had to transform who I would be in our marriage if our relationship was going to survive and prosper. With the Jims of the world, I had to transform who I would be as a consultant if I was going to provide value. In business, we will have to reinvent the meaning of service to others if we are going to survive and prosper.

CHAPTER 2

A BUSINESS AT RISK

In a very real way, we are what we say. Change what we say and we change ourselves and our world. For staff groups, change will be immediate and powerful if they change the conversations they have with customers, senior management, and themselves. Talking about offers and promises is radically different from seeking permission or talking about prescriptions. It is essential that staff groups change their conversations if they are going to transform themselves from functions into successful businesses.

FROM FUNCTION TO BUSINESS

Many staff groups define themselves as functions. As a function, a group bets its survival on the quality of the relationship it forms with senior management rather than on the substance of its contribution to the larger organization. Seeking sanction from those in authority is often more the preoccupation than building the capacity of the organization. Within this framework, there is no more prized achievement than becoming the confidant and extension of powerful people. In pursuit of this end many staff groups become highly skilled at creating intimacy and fostering dependency with senior managers. In this world concepts like customer, banker, and capacity building have little relevance and demand no attention.

There is a fatal flaw in choosing relationship over substance. In the end, responsible managers will abandon a relationship when it is clear that it brings little, if any, value to building the competence of the larger organization. We, who are staff, may experience that moment as betrayal. In fact, it is a responsible and necessary act if a manager is committed to the survival and prosperity of the business. Substance will win out over form. Packaging is really not the point. Being the confidant, offering intimacy without substance, and fostering dependency can not substitute for content or contribution.

The alternative for staff groups is to change before change is forced upon them. To have substance is to master and offer expertise that will build the capacity of the organization to succeed in the marketplace. This is, or should be, the work and purpose of staff groups. It is to forsake the path that seeks sanction and safety through accommodation and patronage. The alternative is choosing to be a *business at risk*. As a business at risk, a staff group faces real competition. Clients within organizations are demanding choice about who provides service. Vendors are knocking at the door. Outsourcing does happen.

Every business at risk has a banker, one or more customers, and an offer.

THE BANKER

Every staff group already has a banker, who has provided assets to create, sustain, and build the staff business. In exchange for those assets, the banker expects something back—what is commonly called a *Return on Investment.* Those who buy stock in a company expect dividends and capital appreciation. Those who lend money expect interest and the return of their principal. *No matter how they measure it, bankers and investors expect greater value in return than they give out.* In banking or the stock market, this transaction is clear and well defined.

Bankers also expect a business to define and conduct itself in the manner in which it is represented to them at the time they invest. This thinking has a broader application and a very useful role to play in redefining the relationship of staff groups to the organization of which they are a part.

THE CORE RESPONSIBILITIES OF THE BANKER

The term *banker* refers to an individual or group who has the responsibility to distribute assets within the organization in service of creating and building the larger business. It is the banker's responsibility to require business units that receive assets to commit to a promise about what they will return in exchange for the use of those assets after a set period of time. The promises are few in number and are stated as results. They may be quantitative or qualitative—whichever is most relevant to the banker. The banker requires that business units explicitly define what they offer their clients. The *primary client* is all the units where the core work of the organization is carried out. This view demands that staff groups be clear about what marketplace they are responsible to and what service or products they are offering. The banker requires business units to choose accountability for their performance by defining consequences for themselves for not keeping promises—before they get the assets. This role is relevant at all levels of an organization. The CEO of a large organization is the banker to the Manufacturing, Distribution, Marketing, and Sales Divisions. A manager of three production teams is the banker to the three teams. A chief of staff responsible for the Finance, Human Resources, and Legal Departments is the banker to all three. Wherever there is a formally recognized team, department, or division that uses assets within an organization, there is a banker with whom that group needs to negotiate promises, offers, and consequences.

This relationship is usually confused within large organizations. It is crystal clear when you are a small business out in the world with no illusion of safety.

When initially asked, "Who is your banker?" internal staff groups look puzzled; for many it is a peculiar question. They frequently conclude that senior management is both their banker and their customer. This seems to be an obvious answer, since staff groups normally exist to serve and act as an extension of senior management. They find it difficult to differentiate the banker from the client.

Bankers and customers are quite different from each other, however. Their interests and demands are divergent.

Conversations with the Banker

Conversations create the world in which we live. To alter what we talk about and how we talk changes the reality we see.

When staff groups think of senior management as bankers, the conversations with them change dramatically. The point is not to get buy-in or secure sponsorship. Staff does not present itself as the agent or extension of senior management seeking permission or direction. Success is not measured by degrees of intimacy achieved. The focus of its conversations moves from relationship to substance.

In negotiating with senior managers as bankers, the point is for staff to be clear and explicit about their offer to the banker, the promises they are eager to make to secure the assets, and the consequences they choose if they fall short. The purpose of the meeting is not to ask permission, but to make promises. All this is not easy. Making promises and choosing consequences can be difficult. It creates vulnerability. This is a very different conversation for staff units. It involves untangling some very old thinking.

The Customer

The key question for a staff group to ask is "Who do we choose as customers?" The primary client is not senior management. It is the work units producing products or providing services to customers. It is the people in the units who actually use the technology staff groups provide. It is to *these* units staff should be accountable.

Just as bankers have specific questions to ask you, so do clients. Just as staff units make a promise to the banker, they need to make an offer and a promise to their clients. It is an offer based on building the competence and capacity of work units. It does not offer prescriptions, mandates, and caretaking. It asks "What is our offer to this work unit about building their capacity to survive and prosper?" or "What is our offer to improve critical results like profitability, cycle time, quality, and giving a unique response in the marketplace?"

Looking at business units as customers, recognizing that staff groups must craft an offer that will build their capacity to succeed, and recognizing that clients have the right to say no are all critical issues in defining a staff group as a business at risk.

CAD/CAM: Bankers and Customers

I recently worked with a group of managers from the CAD/CAM group described in Chapter One. Designers and engineers in the automobile business are absolutely dependent on the technology provided by computer-assisted design (CAD) and computer-assisted management (CAM). Without it they can't do their work. As part of the initial work, I gave the CAD/CAM managers two questions to answer: "Who is your banker?" and "Who is your customer?"

The answers were consistent. Senior managers were their customers. The banker concept was confusing. They didn't understand what it meant for them. They had a narrow view about bankers and customers. At the end of the discussion they concluded, "We are here to serve senior management whatever you want to call them—bankers or customers. Period."

They saw work units, the designers and engineers, not as customers but as subordinates who were expected to comply with policies and practices they had constructed for use of their technology. Their most important responsibility was oversight of the Design and Engineering Departments. "We are representatives of senior management. That's what we do. It's our nature." They didn't see designers and engineers as groups who had a right to say yes or no to their *demands*. The CAD/CAM group produced the only software applications that could be used, controlled all decisions regarding hardware, and decided what technology the designers and engineers could acquire from outside vendors.

In doing all this, they saw themselves as pleasing senior management by keeping tight control, ensuring the use of in-house technology, and making sure that none of the designers and engineers stepped beyond the strict boundaries they defined. When I asked, "And what is your promise to your customer?" the answer that came back was "To make sure we stay on top of and in control of the CAD/CAM technologies and keep the software integrated."

They embraced a policing or auditing role. They knew what was best for the designers and engineers, convinced senior management of their position, and enforced its application.

The designers and engineers had a different view. I asked them, "How pleased are you with what you're getting from the CAD/CAM group?" Universally, they felt frustrated and dissatisfied with the kinds of products and services that were being provided. There was a litany of complaints. As one of the designers put it, "It's hopeless to talk to the CAD/CAM group when we need a certain design capacity and they can't immediately provide it. They simply tell us, 'You'll have to wait.' And yet that particular design capacity is fundamental for us to design vehicles."

The frustration was particularly pointed because outside vendors had developed software that met the designers' needs and was ready for immediate installation. "The CAD/CAM group, universally, and almost without exception, refuses to allow any of these outside vendors into Engineering and Design."

If the CAD/CAM staff chose the Design and Engineering units as their customers, they would see how indefensible their position was. What is the likelihood that the CAD/CAM group could be a successful competitor if they were a business at risk in the open market? No business will survive insisting customers use an inferior product. The Design and Engineering departments were saying "We need this capability now and you can't provide it"—and the CAD/CAM group responded by saying, in essence, "Tough. Stand in line. We'll try to design something with the same capability other vendors can provide today, but it may be six to eighteen months down the road before we get it right."

They didn't feel the least bit *at risk* in taking that stance. It was clear that a day of reckoning was coming. Those clients—Design teams and Engineering teams—that were forced to operate in a marketplace filled with high-stakes risk were not going to tolerate diminished capacity to do their jobs simply because a staff group continued to say no to them. They would soon be knocking at the doorstep of senior management about the urgent need to go to outside vendors for quality products.

The CAD/CAM group was well intentioned, skillful, and energetic. It wanted to do well. Unfortunately, the road to failure is paved with good intentions. The heart of the problem is in failing to discriminate between the banker and the customer. Senior management is not the customer. It does not design and engineer the cars and trucks, but it cares deeply that the cars and trucks are well designed and engineered. The customers are the people who use the technology the staff group offers—engineers and designers. In the end, if the design and engineering work is compromised by poor delivery of CAD/CAM technology, they will forsake loyalty to their own group in favor of a better provider.

Defining management as the customer inevitably leads the staff down such a road. The actual customers—designers and engineers—become hostages; demands are substituted for offers, watching wins out over building capacity, and choice is replaced by mandates. The intent of the CAD/CAM group was to seek safety through sponsorship. It was not to ensure its prosperity by the quality of its offer and performance with its customers. Such a stance leads to very peculiar behaviors. It almost forces staff groups to convince senior managers that those who do the work are incompetent and incapable of knowing what they really need. The free marketplace will not tolerate such a stance.

A HUMAN RESOURCES CASE STUDY: WHO DO WE WORK FOR?

The same point was dramatically made with a Human Resources group with which I recently consulted. During the initial meetings, I was encouraging the group to picture itself as a business at risk and articulate its core offer to the organization. I introduced the concepts of banker and customer.

One senior manager in the group saw Human Resources as having two fundamental offers: First, it was the role of Human

Resources to identify and develop senior managers with the most capacity for future contribution to the larger organization. The second offer of Human Resources was to protect the organization from the remainder of the employees. He saw the rest of the organization, the thousands of other human beings who made up its business units, not as customers, but as *suspects*. It was his view that Human Resources needed to strengthen policies and procedures and to exercise vigilant oversight of the employees to ensure they didn't do things that might damage the best interests of the business. He did not envision Human Resources making an offer to the majority of the people in the organization aimed at building individual and unit capacity. In this framework, the banker and the customer are one and the same.

From this framework more peculiar consequences arise. Work units and individuals seeking to make positive changes are likely to get a jarring response from Human Resources: "We'll decide whether or not the changes that you want to make fit within the limits and constraints that we think are appropriate for you. We know what is best." From this framework employees are not customers but children badly in need of caretaking and prescription. It requires Human Resources to see the employee population as limited in competence and suspect in motivation. A Human Resources function embedded in this viewpoint is only essential and valuable if the majority of the organization is flawed.

This is not the stance of a business at risk seeking success through building the business capacity of its clients. It is the stance of a function seeking survival through the sponsorship of those in authority.

What strikes me is how unlikely it is that any outside business would assume such an attitude in the marketplace. What at-risk independent HR and IS consulting business would ever go into the marketplace, meet with a potential client and take such a stance? How long would any firm taking that position survive?

THE AUDIT CASE STUDY

One of the most difficult groups to apply the banker and client concepts to is Audit. When I started consulting to an Audit group in a manufacturing company, its response was once again much the same as what I already have described. It saw its banker and its customer as the same person. It saw the rest of the organization as targets. Its job was to examine what employees were doing in business units, to uncover violations of financial policies or practices, and to prosecute those responsible—all in the best interest of the company. The mission of the Audit team, as they saw it, was to align the organization with the intentions of senior management and to protect the assets of the corporation.

The Audit team felt little, if any, accountability to those creating products and delivering service. It did feel responsible for overseeing and policing them.

That Audit team was a function—not a business.

In the examples I've given so far, staff groups have defined themselves as functions. Being dedicated to, and the agent of, senior management was the point. Employees are seen as adversaries. Staff groups were responsible for control, making sure employees complied with policy and procedure. They certainly don't see the core workers, or the core work units, as customers to whom an offer and promise of service was demanded.

Agents of Upper Management

A number of years ago I worked with a large manufacturing organization. The Human Resources function was large and powerful. During my tenure there, I witnessed the implementation of a value-based training program. It was created, designed, and implemented by the Human Resources group, which believed it was needed throughout the organization. The group approached senior management to sell the values training and acquire senior management's sponsorship. Senior management bought it and made it mandatory for all employees at the suggestion of the Human Resources staff. This meant employees were required to participate in the program, or else. HR then rolled out the training throughout the organization, *never* inquiring of the business units affected whether this intervention was a good use of their resources and time.

What is wrong with this picture? A staff group not only decides what prescription is good for the entire organization, universally and without exception, but also insists that everyone attend and makes attendance a condition of employment. This is not a group that sees itself as a business at risk in the marketplace. This is not a group that has chosen the organization as its customer.

To get another perspective, picture this Human Resources staff as an outside vendor and ask yourself how they would ever survive in the private sector going out to potential clients saying, "We have a program we want to do. It's the only program we do. We believe it's good for everybody, and our position is that your people have to attend or else lose their jobs"? Words fail to express how untenable that position would be in the competitive marketplace.

WHAT'S MISSING?

As large companies get honest with themselves about issues of cost and benefit, the notion of staff groups spending their time and energy on mandated programs, compliance, and enforcement practices *that they create*, comes under serious scrutiny. Eventually, somebody wonders, "Can anyone make the case as to why mandated programs, auditing teams, and enforcement police are valuable to our business? Or can anyone tell me how they build our ability to be profitable, improve quality, reduce cycle time, or give a unique response in the marketplace?"

For the last five years, in almost every discussion with staff groups, when I ask if anyone can make the business case for such staff activity and show how it adds value to the company, the response is silence. Or serious doubts are raised as to whether this kind of traditional staff focus and activity makes a contribution.

If your behavior and mindset are new to your clients, it should be no surprise when they have challenging questions to ask you.

Faced with this question, some staff groups worry that one day their clients are going to take revenge on them. Their fear is well grounded. Imagine the CAD/CAM staff going to the designers and engineers and saying, "We're going to give you choice about where you source CAD/CAM technology." The designers and engineers would run, not walk, to vendors who offer the products they need.

Imagine Human Resources staff going to business units and saying, "You have been funding these mandated programs that we prescribed for you. From now on, we're going to give you choice about whether you fund them or not." They know that the response in most cases is going to be "Not only no but Hell, no!!"

Suppose a business in financial trouble gets choice about which Finance and Audit team it can use. Suppose, further, that independent firms on the outside are making this offer: "Not only can we do a technical audit and whatever else is required to protect your company assets, we can also teach you how to avoid audit problems in the future. Our goal is to transfer as much of our expertise to you as we can." How different this offer sounds from the usual policing approach offered by many financial staffs. Given a choice, the customer will choose the independent firm because it offers clear help and partnership, rather than prescriptions, mandates, and prosecution.

Frameworks are powerful. Frameworks determine where and how you give attention. Groups that define themselves as traditional staff functions seek a strong relationship to senior management. They establish their credibility and influence by seeking to become the extension of senior management's authority. They see the rest of the organization as the object or target of their mandates, prescriptions, and caretaking. Their survival depends on the sanction of senior management—not on service.

To transform a staff function into a business at risk is to let go of all the safety and security the old framework holds. It is to claim accountability for your own prosperity, fulfillment, and success based on the content of the contribution you make to the business. Attention switches to building the competence and capacity of the business rather than securing a comfortable relationship with those in authority. It is betting the family farm on what you can offer rather than on what you can get from others to ensure safety and comfort.

This is no easy shift. Good intentions and theory falter in the face of experience. My own life is testimony to this. Confronted by Jim in his office, every instinct in me pushed to find a way to please him. Survival ugh pleasing is a deeply embedded response. The traditional stance ᴏ. taff groups—with its upward-serving impulses—is in large part born of the same stuff. It can be camouflaged by theory about "delighting the customer" or the importance of leadership. In the end, it has more to do with my hope that someone else will provide for my comfort, safety, and prosperity. Here are the maxims the job requires:

- Choose to be a business at risk.
- Make senior management the banker.
- Make core work units the customer.
- Change conversations with customers and senior management.
- Give customers choice.

How the Shift Happens

Give line units a choice about where they obtain staff services—Finance, Human Resources, Quality, Information Systems—and any other technology that is critical to them. This step is the single most powerful act for moving staff groups in this direction. *The most powerful way for it to occur is for staff groups themselves to advocate and argue for it.*

There is more to do than just argue for customer choice. Staff groups have to untangle their banker and customer relationships. To do this is to change the conversations with each group. If the conversations don't change, nothing will happen.

CAD/CAM: Changing Conversations

Over time, CAD/CAM rethought its position. "If the designers and engineers really are our customers, what is it they want from us? What's the offer we have to make to be the provider of choice?"

In asking that question, CAD/CAM recognized it hadn't had conversations with these customers about what they wanted and how CAD/CAM could provide technology that built client business capacity. The first step was to enter into those conversations. The next chapter tells the story of how changing the conversations with its customers radically transformed the CAD/CAM group.

Equally important was its recognition that it had been having the wrong conversation with its senior management. Real change started to occur when it changed that conversation as well.

The old conversation with senior management used to start something like this: "We know best what is needed by Design and Engineering. They are 'babes in the woods' when it comes to dealing with outside vendors. They are likely to spend big bucks on programs that don't keep their promise or don't integrate easily with the system already in place. We advise caution, control, and vigilance. You need to take a strong position, supporting our oversight and control of these groups."

In many ways, senior executives have historically liked the notion that staff groups are an extension of their will. Finding it attractive, they haven't had much problem with the prescriptive ways staff groups have operated.

What was required of the CAD/CAM group was nothing less than the education of senior management.

It meant saying to senior management, "We're not sure that, by continuing this prescriptive, compliance-based approach with the rest of the organization, we serve either you, the engineers and designers, or ourselves well. We don't believe we're currently making the best use of our expertise to build capacity in the organization. In the longer run, we think we need to see ourselves more as a capacity-building function and less as a police function. Serious questions are being raised about the value of all this focus on compliance and prescription and how such an approach affects outcomes this company cares about, like profitability, product, and uniqueness in the marketplace."

In a very real sense, the CAD/CAM staff had to initiate the transformation of senior management into bankers, rather than wait for senior management to do it. One might wish senior executives would initiate the needed changes in the conversation and the relationship, but the reality is they are not likely to do so unless and until staff groups move toward changing it themselves.

The second step in the education of upper management was to say, "We think both you and we should, in the future, define CAD/CAM as a business at risk. We think the way we need to be seen—because it is the reality—is as a business in competition with many other businesses out there wanting to provide the same service to our designers and engineers. We believe that if we as an organization move toward giving our internal customers choice about how they source their CAD/CAM services, we will be challenged to be the best we can be."

Finally, the conversation focuses on promises. "What's the promise you want fulfilled in return for the assets you're extending to us? We want to get as clear as we can about the promise, and be as straight as we can with you about whether we think we can fulfill it. It's also important that our promise to you makes sense in relationship to what we want to promise our customers and the capacity we're trying to build in them."

It's not at all unusual in these initial conversations for a senior manager with all the good will in the world to say, "Stop! I'm confused. Why are you talking about loosening the controls? What do you mean, 'What's the promise I want fulfilled in exchange for the assets I extend to you?' We have a good working relationship—you do to the employees what we tell you to do. What's there to change?"

CAD/CAM didn't ask permission. It made offers and promises. It didn't ask for sponsorship. It chose risk. It was not intent on convincing senior management of the need for more oversight and audit of the Design and Engineering groups. It argued for customer choice. It didn't seek a safe future through sanction. It sought a future based on the quality of their contribution to the doing of the work.

IN CONCLUSION

To choose to be a business at risk is an act of courage. It is to give up the safety that the old relationship offered. It is about choosing to be at risk as an act of service to the organization. To give up safety and embrace risk in the marketplace—to enthusiastically take that position—does not come easily. And yet, to try to maintain the protected position is a prescription for eventual suicide. The free marketplace will win out.

THE PLAYING FIELD

It's easy to espouse a theory, and much harder to see how to translate it into day-to-day operations. Take a break from reading and think about the questions in this section, which any staff function will find useful in defining itself as a business at risk. Chapters Three and Four will give additional help with the questions if the concepts still seem hard to grasp.

Begin by adopting these assumptions—provisionally, if necessary:

- The clients are the core work units of the organization.
- The goal is transfer of expertise that will build the capacity of clients to deliver on their promises to their customers and bankers.
- The method of delivery is customization through collaborative consultation.
- The funding vehicle is charge back.

In light of these assumptions, how would you answer the following questions for your organization:

What is the expertise to which we lay claim? What are the products and services we have created that use this expertise?

Using our expertise, what is the offer we make to clients that will result in enhanced capacity to increase profitability, improve quality, shorten cycle times, and differentiate themselves in the marketplace?

What is the guarantee we choose to offer?

Who is our competition and what makes their offer unique and attractive to the client?

What makes our offer preferable to others who make a similar offer?

Who is our banker? What is the promise we need to make to sustain support in the future?

What are the constraints we must honor and respect in doing our business?

What is the single most difficult issue we face with:

- Bankers?
- Clients?
- Ourselves?

CHAPTER 3

OFFERS, PROMISES, AND GUARANTEES

When a staff group defines itself as a business at risk, the conversations it conducts with its clients necessarily change. Instead of relationships, conversations begin to focus on offers, promises, and guarantees.

This chapter is about offers. For staff groups, the heart of an authentic offer is a promise to use the best expertise available to build the capacity and competence of a client unit to prosper in the marketplace. The point is not to control the clients—not to prescribe for them, not to mandate. A credible and compelling offer embraces accountability for having impact on business outcomes.

FALSE OFFERS

Many staff postures masquerade as offers to clients. Making demands and holding the client hostage do not constitute offers. Both of these were discussed in the previous chapter. This section describes other versions of offers that fail the test of "a promise to build capacity."

WANTING A PLACE AT THE TABLE AND A PARTNERSHIP

I recently witnessed a meeting between the managers of several line organizations and the managers of the staff groups. The meeting was aimed at resolving ongoing conflict between the staff and line departments. People were on edge. Central to the staff complaints was the perception that they were being excluded from key meetings within the line departments. One of the senior Finance managers seemed particularly determined, "You've asked what we want. I don't know about my peers, but I can speak for myself. I want a place at the table. I want to be there when decisions are made. I want partnership with the line departments."

One of the line managers responded, "Look, Sue, everyone wants a place at the table. What do you bring to the table? Why should you get the seat?"

"What I am offering, Bill, is partnership and a willingness to learn about the business from your perspective. I think that's reason enough to be invited to be there," Sue replied.

"Please don't take me wrong, but it is not enough reason for me to invite you in. I want to know what you are bringing to the table besides curiosity about the business and some wish to be my partner," Bill answered. "How are you going to help get us another customer or increase our margins? That's the kind of people I need at the table. If you want to be a so-called partner you've got to bring something that makes a difference. What is it, Sue?"

"That's the answer I expected from you, Bill," Sue retorted. "The truth is you don't want me or us there because we don't report to you and you can't own us!"

"Well, maybe there is some truth in that, Sue, but that's not what I'm talking about right now. I'm talking about everyone in my organization being under the gun to demonstrate the value of their contribution. Why should it be any different for you? Wanting partnership is just not enough. Partnership without substance isn't going to cut it in my organization."

I believe Bill was fundamentally right. One might hope that truth is always expressed with compassion. Sometimes it comes in harsher forms. So be it. Frequently staff groups don't want to see the truth in its harsh or soft form. Translating the complaints of clients into "control" issues or into some form of "resistance" is a good way to miss the point.

A credible offer demands a promise of positive impact. Partnership demands substantive contribution. Relationship by itself is not enough.

GOALS, OBJECTIVES, AND ACTIVITIES

If you ask many staff groups to tell you what their offer is, frequently they will talk about their goals and objectives for the year. Typically, Human Resources lists items like reducing training costs, rolling out a program, or carrying out a set of standard annual activities such as attitude surveys. Often part of the offer is to monitor and make sure that performance reviews are completed, succession planning gets done, and that people sign up and attend mandated programs. To HR staff, the list of goals and objectives constitutes the offer they make to the organization.

But does that constitute an offer to build competence and capacity in the organization?

No. It constitutes a list of activities Human Resources is going to carry out. There is no mention of business outcomes.

As so many managers do, I would find activity lists irrelevant if I'm worried about lowering unit cost and cutting cycle time. The Human Resources annual program of activities has no relationship to me. The program may be relevant to the Human Resources staff, but as their client, my response to them is "So what's your point? Why should I find what you're proposing to do about succession planning or workshop programs a credible and compelling offer? I hear nothing about your promising to solve the concrete cost and quality problems I'm facing."

> *You can continue to do what you are doing now. Or you can adopt a different intention. You have a choice at this moment to move in a new direction.*

Forcing clients to select from or participate in a schedule of programs is a very different act from choosing risk in the marketplace by saying, "Here's what I have to offer to build your business. Are you interested?"

NEEDS ASSESSMENTS

If you challenge staff groups on the questionable relevance of their activities to the client, they'll often respond, "Well, we can't talk about an offer until we do a needs assessment." In other words, the immediate offer is to do a needs assessment.

If there is one thing business units don't need, it's another needs assessment. A needs assessment is not an offer. It can camouflage the absence of a substantive offer. An offer doesn't come in the form of a question; it comes in the form of a statement. It has content. To make an offer requires mastery of expertise—theories and methods—with the power to improve business results. Before entering into any conversation with a client I must know what I have to offer in clear and simple terms. I must be able to explain my expertise and make it relevant to the client's business results.

The line units seldom get from staff groups an offer to build business competence and capacity. Staff rarely say, "Here's the technology we have that we think can build your business and improve your results."

True, at the moment, neither the staff nor the clients know how that technology applies to a specific set of circumstances. An assessment or discovery process may need to follow—but they are not the offer itself. It is the work of staff groups to know what their offer is before they ever reach the client's office and before they propose a needs assessment.

CRAFTING A CREDIBLE AND COMPELLING OFFER

An authentic offer is not a set of goals and objectives, a list of mandated programs, a needs assessment, or a menu of activities. What is it?

A compelling and credible offer is a promise to use the best expertise available to build the capacity and competence of client units to prosper in the marketplace. The promise is backed by a guarantee.

A compelling offer has three components: expertise, relevance, and accountability.

The first component of the offer is *expertise,* what a staff group brings to the table. Expertise is a set of theories and methods that can make a difference to business outcomes. Without mastery of an expertise, staff groups have nothing to offer.

The second component is *relevance.* This means staff can make clear to the client how the application of expertise can improve the capacity of a business to make it in the marketplace. When I say "make clear," I mean being able to take a very specific, simple, and clear application of technology and show how it can be applied with business benefit—impact on results. It means tying application of technology to real business outcomes like profitability, quality, cycle time, and customer satisfaction.

If I were talking to a client about my own offer, I might put these two elements together this way:

Expertise. "My technology creates business literacy throughout an organization. I know how to design systems and convene meetings that build and sustain business literacy."

Relevance. "I believe that if you move toward distributing literacy throughout your organization, it will directly improve the way employees respond to customers, suppliers, and one another. The more literate they are, the more powerful their response will be to everyone they come in contact with. If you can treat each customer in a personalized way, it will improve profitability and customer satisfaction."

Freely choosing *accountability* for these business outcomes is the last component of an offer. To make a credible and compelling offer means to tie myself to business outcomes. It is the language of promises and guarantees.

CHOOSING ACCOUNTABILITY

Choosing accountability for outcomes makes a credible offer compelling.

There are three attitudes a staff group can take toward accountability for outcomes: to avoid it, to be held accountable by the client, or to freely choose to be accountable.

Those who would like to avoid accountability for business outcomes tell their clients, "I'll come and do my workshops but I can make no promises. There are too many variables I can't control." Showing up is enough.

In the second position, the staff group is willing to be held accountable by the client. Service promises are given cautiously and only when demanded by the client. There is endless and tedious discussion of measures.

In contrast, making a compelling offer is choosing to be accountable for improving business outcomes through applying technology. I demand it of myself. I insist on it with a client. I make it a condition of working with a client.

Accountability is sticky stuff. "Holding others accountable" or "being held accountable" are the forms with which most of us are familiar. In most organizations, holding others accountable is seen as a virtue. It is something good leaders know how to do. It is the justification for all the vigilant watching carried out by managers and staff groups. However noble it may be, it has a downside. Basing organizational life on vigilance is expensive both in dollars and time. Watching is not a particularly productive posture when you're trying to get something out the door. The other caution I have about a "holding accountable" attitude is that it indicates surrender to a negative view of human beings. It implies that people will not be responsible unless they are caught and prosecuted. It's their nature.

This book embodies a different assumption. In each of us resides not only the capacity but the will and desire to choose accountability for our lives and actions. Some part of each of us wants to make a contribution to the world. Some part of each of us wants to create meaning and worth in our lives by taking stances based on values and not barter or the promise of a return. From this stance I focus on what I offer to the world, not on what I get back from it. From this stance I confess my own responsibility rather than look for others to blame.

I have struggled in my life with these issues, both personally and professionally. Some piece of me desperately wants innocence and comfort. Choosing accountability requires embracing guilt and forsaking comfort. I have been pointedly asked, "What's the payoff for doing this? Why should anybody take this road? Get real!" I ask myself the same questions. My answer to myself and to others is twofold. I want to live a life in which I can believe. I want to take a stance based on the worth of my work. I want the point to be the contribution it makes.

I also believe it is good for business. The most powerful stance I can take with a client is to focus on an offer, committing to improving results and insisting on accountability for keeping promises. Here are the key steps:

- *Lay claim to an expertise.*
- *Connect the use of expertise to business results.*

- *Construct a compelling business argument for using it.*
- *Insist on promises and guarantees based on results.*
- *Advocate for client choice.*

CHANGING THE CONVERSATIONS WITH CLIENTS

Making a genuine offer is very different from talking about demands, mandates, needs assessments, lists of activities, or relationships for their own sake. It is saying clearly to a client, "This staff group wants to be accountable for the application of its technology in your business. In fact, it is a condition we insist upon. We choose to be accountable to improve business outcomes in your unit, and we expect there to be consequences if we don't."

It is the right conversation.

How does a staff group apply this thinking in practical terms to the crafting of an offer?

ANOTHER HUMAN RESOURCES CASE STUDY: GETTING STARTED

Of all the staff groups, Human Resources may face the most difficult challenge in constructing a credible and compelling offer. This was particularly apparent in an organization I worked with recently, a large metropolitan newspaper. It was willing to let go of old activities as a basis for an offer but became stymied in the process of constructing a new one. The difficult issue was the inability to identify a Human Resources technology that could be directly connected to business outcomes.

It was so difficult for the Human Resources group that June, the manager of the group, called me to discuss it. "When I look at the people we have in the Human Resources unit now, and when I look at the shift we have to make to present a credible offer to this organization, I am tempted to lose hope. I can list the activities we do, but take those away from us, and I don't see what our expertise can possibly be. Do we even have an expertise? I don't see us having the skills we need to make a genuine offer. If that weren't difficult enough, I'm not sure that I or the people on my team have enough flexibility and willingness to transform ourselves to master new and unfamiliar skills. We are used to being protected and safe." She added, "For me to move in this direction means to raise serious issues about who will be staying on staff and who will not fit in here anymore."

She was tough minded enough to recognize the implications of this change and what it required to make a compelling offer and what it meant to be at risk. She had understandable concern that loyal people, people who showed up every day and did their work, stood in jeopardy of losing their jobs.

Moving to this new stance is not merely an intellectual exercise. It means asking serious questions about whether you and your group have the capacity to embrace it and live it out.

She chose to proceed. "The first thing we need to do is go to our clients and say, 'For the Human Resources Department to be credible with you, we have to make an offer to improve the results of your unit. Whether you are in circulation, advertising, production or the news room, we want to be accountable. If we can't do that, we shouldn't be here.'"

When I asked her if she knew what outcomes the various units in the newspaper cared about, she was clear. "In advertising, they care about revenue. In circulation, they care about how many papers and subscriptions they sell and how quickly they can get the paper out. In production, they worry about costs. In the newsroom, they care intensely about the quality of the journalism and the value of a free press. If we can't contribute to those outcomes, we don't belong here."

She went to each of these client departments and said, "Here's where we think we must have impact in your department if Human Resources is going to make a difference." She spelled out what she saw as the concerns of each department.

She then said to them, "At present, we don't have the capacity to do that. I can't make you a promise that we can affect these factors, because we don't have the expertise to do it."

She continued, "I'm asking you to give us a period of time to get our act together while we move toward developing this expertise internally. If, after six months, we can't provide the impact you have a right to expect from HR, the dollars that we now use within Human Resources should be used to source the expertise you need, even if that costs us our jobs." She embraced the heart of accountability.

To the employees of Human Resources she said, "In this new world, each one of us is at risk. If we can't develop the technology to make an offer that has real impact on the outcomes our clients care about, we shouldn't be here." Next, she said, "For each of us, the question is 'How willing are we to learn? How willing are we to change what we know how to do, so that we can make a legitimate offer that has real credibility and promise for our customers?'"

REDEFINING ONE'S EXPERTISE

This Human Resources group became a business at risk. They recognized the necessity of crafting an offer to build capacity, but they also recognized that they were unequipped to make such an offer and carry it out.

HUMAN RESOURCES: DEFINING THE BUSINESS

In subsequent discussions within the staff group, members concluded they were really running two businesses. In one business, they managed transactions like payroll, benefits, and employment. In the other business they consulted. The consulting business required a sophisticated expertise capable of affecting business results of clients. A hard look at the transaction business led to outsourcing it based on cost, quality, and other key measures.

What remained was for staff members to turn themselves into a source of expertise that would help their organization. They are now in the process of redefining what their expertise is and what their offer will be.

CAD/CAM: BUILDING AN OFFER

Once the CAD/CAM group had differentiated its banker from its clients, it was faced with forging an offer to its clients.

"This is something we've never done before," they said. "To see designers and engineers as our clients, to take a position advocating that they get choice about whom they use as a source for their technical software needs." They wondered, "What constitutes the right offer?"

At one point, one of the managers voiced what everyone realized: "Our offer has to ensure the best possible technology, the best possible software for designers and engineers to do their work. This commitment is at the center. Our key expertise is not being a software company but providing the best software that is available to our Design and Engineering groups—no matter where it comes from."

"What are the implications of that?" they asked themselves.

"It means we have to stop seeing outside vendors as the enemy," someone replied. "We should see them as allies we can collaborate with to build a library of software for designers and engineers."

It was a revolutionary step.

The staff members grasped that they had customers to serve—the company's designers and engineers—whom they had never really embraced as customers. They recognized that their preoccupation with control and creating a software company was irrelevant to the customers. They came to the conclusion that their business had changed from software development to sourcing and integration.

Vendors who had been their competition were redefined as allies. For years, they had been the enemy. "Keep the door closed. Don't allow them on the grounds. Keep them out of contact with the designers and engineers." Now the question became "How do we invite them in so we can integrate their products and services into our overall offer?"

The shift in position was profound. The definition of the group's expertise had changed from creating, promoting, and protecting its own software production rights to sourcing and integrating state-of-the-art software for its customers.

To claim ownership of clients, to prescribe for clients, to claim sole responsibility for developing all the software clients would need is not practical in the world of technology today. This group's original sense of owning the client gave way to providing for the client the best available expertise, no matter where it came from. Before, CAD/CAM had seen the integration of these inside and outside technologies as something that created problems. It justified its "no" to the outside vendors by saying, "Their software won't integrate easily into the overall CAD/CAM technology used by the Design and Engineering groups." Now it saw software integration as a problem *it* had to solve in the interest of the client.

At the end, some members of the group struggled with recasting vendors as allies. It was painful. "You want us to look at vendors, who have been criticizing our software and appealing to the Design and Engineering units behind our backs, as people with whom we should now collaborate? That's going to be very difficult." It didn't go down easily.

The CAD/CAM group came to terms with the shift when it recognized that being prescriptive with the client or being focused on creating an internal software development company were all irrelevant distractions. The designers and the engineers kept repeating their request, "All we want, all we ever wanted, is the best available technology."

Redefinition required conversion in the CAD/CAM group. That change demonstrated itself in the new offer they crafted. First, they laid claim to an expertise and a technology. Next, they developed presentations that made the application of these technologies relevant to the design and engineering process. Finally, they showed how these applications contributed to design possibilities.

THE FINANCE CASE STUDY

When Finance groups talk about their offer, what they often mean is "We get reports out the door on time" or "We gather data" or "We carry out monitoring and compliance activities" or "We manage company planning activities." They believe that if they oversee the budget and if reports arrive at the right time, they've succeeded. Doing activities is a popular measure of success in almost all staff groups.

Is getting reports out on time a sufficient measure of success? If we are a business at risk faced with tough competition, an offer based on doing activities seems something less than compelling.

The Finance staff at a manufacturing plant was faced with strong outside competition. Its vague offer paled in comparison to outside firms whose offers were clear, compelling, and credible. The independent firms were not just promising to get the reports out on time, they were also promising to provide additional services for the same price.

They made bold promises. "We can broaden business literacy throughout your organization by redesigning your financial reports so that people at all levels of the organization can read the numbers and see how they can improve results. We can respond rapidly to situations where you need a unique financial measure."

With outside competition beating at their door, the Finance staff at the plant had to struggle with two difficult questions:

- If our core technology in Finance is creating useful measures that lead to good business decisions, how do we offer that expertise in a way that competes successfully with the offer outside vendors are making? How do we put together a better offer?

- If we want to make an offer to the units we serve, an offer that clearly affects business outcomes, how do we state it? How do we differentiate ourselves from vendors making a similar offer?

Reality struck. "It's not just getting the reports out on time. It's how those reports are used." "It's great for *us* to understand what the numbers mean and how they relate to each other, but if we can't create that same financial literacy throughout the organization, we really haven't achieved much."

As the Finance people began to redefine themselves, they started to change the conversations with the business units, "We want to transfer our technology broadly in your unit to create increased self-sufficiency. These skills can be used to make informed decisions throughout your business rather than having a few executives literate about what the numbers mean or having your unit depend on us for interpretation."

The Finance staff members suddenly saw themselves as consultants out to create business literacy within their client units. Success would be measured by the literacy that they created and the better business decisions that would follow. They had connected expertise, application, and business outcomes in a clear and concise way. They chose accountability for impact. They had created an *offer.*

AN ORGANIZATION IN CRISIS

I recently worked with a major newspaper publishing business that was in the midst of a serious financial and marketing crisis. Revenues had been declining for several years. Costs were increasing dramatically. The customer base was flat.

Only a few people at the top knew how serious the problem was. They had known it for months. They had to deal with it.

When I asked, "Who is going to go out and tell people about this problem? Who understands it well enough to be able to explain it?" the difficulty of the situation became evident. If what was demanded was a sophisticated understanding of the problem, its causes, the issues involved, their implications, and the ability to answer questions, perhaps three people in the organization were qualified—the head of Finance, the CEO, and the COO of the company. If doomsday is fast approaching and if you're going to inform two thousand people about a complex financial problem, three people can't do it.

After a great deal of discussion, the Finance staff chose to make itself central to resolving the issue. The head of Finance concluded, "Given this crisis and these circumstances, it is not enough to tell people, 'We've got a multimillion dollar problem, what are you going to do about it?' If the strategy is to inform the whole organization, to make it business literate in hopes of everyone better managing the situation, we have the expertise to do that. We are the people here who understand and can best explain the problem."

The Finance staff chose accountability for developing a way to explain this problem to the general population. It made an offer to the organization, "We'll do three things: First, we'll put together documentation about the origins and history of this problem, what it means in these circumstances, and what the future of the organization would be based on different scenarios."

"Second, we will train middle managers and supervisors to present all this information and answer questions about it. In other words, we will transfer our understanding of the situation to them, so that they can work with their units and sustain literacy as this crisis unfolds over time."

The second promise ensured a greatly increased resource in the organization for explaining and managing the issues.

The third offer was for a member of the Finance staff to be present at the meetings as a resource to help deal with questions that were particularly complex.

In only a few days, Finance staff members developed a simple one-hour presentation that made sense of this problem to everyone. Next, they trained seventy-five middle managers and supervisors to deliver this message to the various departments and work units. They provided them with handouts. They formulated answers to typical questions employees might have. They trained the presenters to give the presentation. Finally, they showed up to deal with some of the unique questions that arose when the presentations were made.

It was a radical redefinition of a traditional Finance function. from "All we're accountable for is to turn out standard financial reports for senior management" to "We are accountable for creating in the organization a widespread understanding of this problem. We believe that widespread understanding will lead to more intelligent action and ownership of the problem throughout the organization."

What was the business outcome? The entire organization mobilized to focus on critical issues because Finance had laid claim to its expertise, demonstrated the relevance of its application in this crisis, and tied that application to business outcomes. It helped create an organization where everyone could focus on the difficult issue and devote energy to its resolution.

The Finance staff members made an offer to use their technology to improve business outcomes. What they did was take a position and in so doing make a statement: "We want to put ourselves on the line about creating business literacy throughout this newspaper. We choose to be accountable for the impact of this action on business outcomes. We expect there will be consequences to us if we don't build the capacity of the organization to deal with this crisis." No one demanded they put themselves into the center of the crisis; they chose to stand on that ground. It was a radical act of redefinition and a far cry from the former offer of "Let's just get the reports out."

Promises and Guarantees

In issuing a guarantee and a promise, I tie myself to something tangible.

For many years one of my most attractive distractions from doing consulting work was dreaming of building my own woodworking shop. After discussing, delaying, debating, and deliberating about it, I finally built it. The shop made a difference in my life and taught me a number of lessons about working. I found it satisfying to work in my shop, with its saws, drills, planes, and hand tools. It provided an experience missing in my professional life—a sense of satisfaction upon completing something I could hold in my hands. The satisfaction of doing consulting work never equaled the satisfaction I got from creating a chest, a box, or a table. I found myself rushing from the airport back to my home in Vermont—and as soon as I had said hello to my family, I was off to the woodworking shop.

I thought more and more about the difference between the quality of my consulting experience and the quality of my experience in the shop. Things concrete and tangible came out of that woodworking shop. I would begin a project with pieces of rough wood. With time and substantial effort, I made a product—a box, a chest, a table. I could look at it, touch it, and put it somewhere. I had achieved a result, albeit not perfect, but a result in which I took satisfaction.

In contrast, I found no such satisfaction when I examined my professional life. The experience of completion was absent. "Why do I feel so unsatisfied?" I asked myself. "I spend 150 days a year flying all over the country, leading workshops and consulting with clients, I should be proud. Why, then, do I feel so deeply unsatisfied?"

In woodworking, there was always a moment when my efforts resulted in some public outcome that could be seen and touched and felt. In my consulting work, on the other hand, I was someone performing a series of activities. I was getting paid for showing up and conducting a workshop or doing a consulting process. I had defined my work as "showing up and performing an activity." True enough, the activity itself could go well or poorly. People would like the workshop or they wouldn't. People would feel that my consulting advice was useful or not. But in a real sense it was a shallow outcome. After delivering a three-day workshop, I measured my success by how people felt about it. In my heart, even when people said, "We really enjoyed your workshop," I didn't find it particularly satisfying. They seldom made comments like "What you've done here is really important and here's how it will make a difference in results." When I left, I could not touch or feel anything. There was no definitive way to discriminate between success and failure. There was nothing I could take particular pride in and say, "This is what I accomplished. This is what I built today."

> *If the service industry is to survive and thrive in today's marketplace, it must be able to present itself as able to help organizations meet the business demands they face.*

OTHER DOUBTS

I always envied line managers because their outcomes were clear and measurable. They knew if they failed or succeeded; they could measure it. At the end of three months or a year, what their efforts had come to and what impact they had had was public. The measure might be market share, profitability, or management earnings. Whatever the measure, something clearly had been achieved—or not achieved—that had real impact on a business.

I clearly didn't have that experience. Feedback about how well people liked my workshop was in no way the equivalent measure of success received by line managers at risk in a marketplace, who had to develop customers, be accountable for profitability, and resolve serious issues of survival. I couldn't correlate my workshop performance in any direct way with impact on results.

Economic issues added to my doubts. Even though I would talk solemnly with other consultants about the importance of "our work" and how deeply committed and filled with purpose we were, inside I was primarily driven by my own economic need. Was I going to bill enough days this month or this year to pay the mortgage, send the kids to college, and put something away for retirement? At some level, I was simply scheduling my show to play as often as I could. Since I was my own booking agent, I found myself promoting my workshops in order to schedule days.

I didn't talk about it. I suspected it went on with others, but they didn't talk about it. One doesn't have to wonder why.

RESOLUTION

When I took account of the doubts, the problem was clear: "I don't trust the work I'm doing. I have little conviction that it does anything for the results of the organizations I serve."

This conclusion became particularly painful to me when I started to move toward the position I've presented in the preceding chapters. I was advocating that staff people put themselves at risk in the marketplace, make offers with value to clients, choose for accountability, share and bear financial consequences with their clients. Yet in my own consulting work, what was I personally putting on the line? Was I willing to take the same risk that I was telling clients they ought to be taking? Was I willing to put myself on the line in the same way I was advocating for others? It's one thing to talk about choosing accountability and risk, clearly another thing to do it.

MY FIRST STEPS

My initial attempts at resolving this issue were passive. I encouraged clients to hold me accountable for outcomes they cared about.

In taking that position, I expected them to raise difficult issues with me if I didn't produce the promised outcomes. The responsibility remained with them to do the work of holding me accountable.

It didn't work. Perhaps they didn't know how to do it. Perhaps my words said I wanted to hear the difficult issues while my whole bearing said I didn't. When clients didn't call me to task on difficult issues, I could always blame them: "I would have been willing to be held accountable if they had been willing to hold me accountable."

I stayed with this passive stance for a long time, believing that I was being accountable. A lingering dissatisfaction remained. I still didn't feel I was making a real impact on things that were important to my clients.

Finally, I realized I didn't have to wait for someone else to hold me accountable. If I wanted accountability, I could choose it. I could hold myself accountable. Another voice in me argued against such a rash act. "In consulting work outcomes are vague and you don't control all the variables." I had to let go of that excuse. The daring act is to choose for accountability and make it a condition of working with a client.

To give meaning to my work, to believe in what I was doing, I had to somehow embrace and demand this risk.

The radical act for me was to be able to initiate a conversation with a client in which I said, "One of the conditions of my working with you is that I be accountable for how I affect business outcomes here. I need your help to define what this means, but it's something that's got to be an explicit part of our contract. Before we start to work together, not only do I want to choose for accountability about outcomes, I want to establish consequences if I don't produce what I promise. I want it to be clear that I have something at stake if I fail to fulfill promises I make to you."

A Double-Edged Sword

All this didn't come easily. Choosing accountability for my life and work has not been at the top of my To-Do list. Yet the thought persisted. "Be who you can be in this world, Joel. It's up to you. Nobody is going to make you choose accountability. It's been clear you've gotten away without anybody forcing you to do it for years. If you want to be accountable, demand it of yourself."

The choice to walk this road is made in the face of doubt and uncertainty. "My God, do I really want to choose for accountability, issue a guarantee, and define consequences? Suppose I can't produce? Suppose it all falls short?"

Feeling this double-edged sword was profound for me. On one side was fear of failure and on the other was the attraction of taking a stance in the world—committing to substance and impact.

Being committed to outcomes changed the nature of how clients responded to me. I was taken more seriously because I took myself more seriously.

Understanding Cynicism

Staff people in organizations hear a familiar criticism from people in line units, "Those who can—do; those who can't—take staff jobs." Human Resources people are often cynically characterized as "touchy feely people" having little relevance. Finance staff are labeled "bean counters." Systems people are categorized as "techies" or "nerds" with little business knowledge. These criticisms of staff are voiced because of what's missing in the work we do and the offer we make. The missing element is our willingness to make the commitment, to choose risk, to voluntarily tie ourselves to outcomes and consequences.

Putting It on the Line

A number of years ago I had the opportunity to work with the international division of a large American manufacturing business. The leader of the organization, Rick, became one of my most valued teachers. He fully understood the issue of accountability.

The international operation was struggling badly. Major amounts of capital were being invested in it with a poor return. Rick called a meeting in San Francisco for all senior managers from the various countries and regional operations of the company.

He didn't open the meeting by saying, "We're in trouble, and how are we going to survive as an organization?" He didn't open with "Let's do some chipping around costs so we can at least show some improvement." Neither did he open the conversation by complaining about poor monetary exchange rates and other reasons why performance was bad.

He opened the meeting by saying, "At the end of this year, I'm going to recommend to the CEO one of two courses of

action: either that he continue to fund the international operation based on our achieving the expected rate of return on his
investments, or that he liquidate his capital investment in
international operations and invest those funds somewhere
where the promise of a return is kept. What's on the line for us
is whether or not I, as a leader, and we, as a group, choose to be
accountable about our promise to the company. I want us to
choose the consequences if we can't produce the results. It is our
choice. I, for one, will not live in an organization that produces
mediocre or poor results and expects funding year after year
after year. I choose to take a position that unless we can radically change our financial performance, we choose to go out of
business."

It was the quality of that act that demanded my attention. It was a
unique act on the part of a senior manager to move beyond self-interest
in defining a promise, a guarantee, and a consequence.

STAFF GROUP EXAMPLES

How does this translate into staff groups coming to terms with putting
themselves on the line by issuing a promise and a guarantee? How do
they go about choosing consequences for failure?

HUMAN RESOURCES: CHOOSING CONSEQUENCES

One of the most explicit examples is the one I cited earlier about
the head of Human Resources at the newspaper. Her guarantee
was to say to the line managers, "If I don't produce value and
improve what you care about in explicit and measurable ways,
I believe the assets now committed to Human Resources ought
to be applied in ways that are useful to you. I can't justify the
funding of this Human Resources department, the headcount
we carry, and the financial support we take from you, if we can't
make some measurable and substantial impact on our business.
It no longer makes sense to me for us just to be here. Showing
up for work is not enough for us anymore. Doing activities is not
enough. You are going to evaluate whether you received value
from us as it was promised. If not, the guarantee is we are going

to convert those funds that pay our salaries into funds that will provide the resources you need. I want you to know, before we begin to go down this road, that this is the consequence I choose for Human Resources. This is nothing you have to hold me accountable for. It's my choice. I'm not going to run a Human Resources staff that doesn't have substance or impact."

It was an extraordinary act of courage on her part to define her organization as a business at risk, to make her guarantee public.

CAD/CAM: Choosing Consequences

The CAD/CAM group had to confront the same issue. Its manager took a tough stand near the end of a particularly difficult discussion, "If we are not able to provide the best available CAD/CAM technology for designers and engineers in a way that directly and immediately improves the quality of our company's products, then I fully expect the company to look outside this group for it. I would insist on it. There will come a day of reckoning when we are going to choose to answer the question: Are we the best providers of the world-class technology that our company needs to be competitive in the marketplace in the decades ahead? If we are still found wanting, I fully expect to move toward sourcing everything Design and Engineering needs from some better provider. Our business is on the line. Whether we survive or not is in our hands. If we can source and create the world-class technology the company needs, we'll be just fine. If we can't, we won't be here."

IN CONCLUSION

Each of these leaders resolved the personal struggle I have described. All of them said in their own words, "I will not live in a world where I make excuses, find reasons to avoid a concrete promise, and justify my value doing activities with no relation to business outcomes."

Offering a promise and a guarantee is the step where this approach moves away from abstract discussions of process, procedure, and method. The issue becomes personal. All the managers I have discussed not only put their groups at risk but also put themselves at risk. They neither asked for nor claimed an exemption from the consequences of their decisions.

The alternative is to search for the easy path. Traditionally we have rationalized and built intellectual, defensive arguments to excuse us from accountability. The arguments are endless. We may claim that results of our service activities are not definable in terms of outcomes to the business, or we may claim that we only have measurable impact over an extended period of time. We may say the effects of our activities are very subtle and hard to measure. Or we may claim it's the activity we do that counts, not its consequences on the business. We may blame the clients. "If only the clients had acted the way they should have acted and done what we told them to do, then we would have had more effect on their business." Or "I can't be accountable for business outcomes because I don't control them." You get the point.

We in staff positions have crafted these arguments to excuse ourselves from the pain of accountability. I have used all those same empty arguments myself. These excuses embody our doubts and fears.

We live in a world where substance and results count. Packaging is not the point. Form will not win out over substance. As staff people, we can't hide any longer in a place of safety far from the harsh reality of the marketplace. A day of reckoning is at hand when we will be called to account for what we produce for the business and what happens to business results because of our efforts. Hiding will not work. The issue isn't to build the walls higher or nail the doors tighter. The issue isn't to find some road to safety and greater security. The way out of this is *through* it.

As staff, we must put ourselves at risk by choosing to be accountable for business outcomes and demonstrating in our offer that we have an expertise that can change them.

You now know you have a choice. Rather than spending your energy managing relationships, reducing tension, and defusing emotions, you can make an offer and guarantee for your client's success.

Paradoxically, the way to survival today is to choose risk by making an offer in the marketplace, promising to improve results, and living with the consequences of performance.

Chapter 4

STANCE AND EXPERTISE

Staff groups rarely think about the use of their technology, yet it is one of the most serious questions they face. Finance, Information Systems, Human Resources, Quality, and Engineering all know how to do certain things, how to use theory and methods to produce results. This expertise can be used in ways that build competence in a client or in ways that don't. The client can either use or misuse staff technology. Because of this, it is critical for staff groups to have a point of view about the appropriate use of their expertise.

Teaching and the practice of medicine illustrate the point. Elementary school teachers may be masters of their profession. They may know a dozen different approaches to teaching math and reading. They may have a genius for motivating young children. If parents don't create the conditions at home that support their efforts, the learning will be limited at best. The full value of the teacher's expertise is only realized when parents take time to read with their children, support discipline about homework, and positively reinforce good performance. How the family uses the teacher's expertise makes a critical difference in the final outcomes.

Doctors have all kinds of expertise to solve problems like obesity and hypertension. Their technology will only work if the patient chooses to create the conditions that support it. Continuing to smoke, drink, and overeat will surely lead to failure of the best medical interventions. All this is obvious with doctors and teachers. It may not be as obvious in other service professions, but it is just as true. If clients are not willing to create the conditions that support the use of staff expertise, there is little hope for success. It is the responsibility of the staff to define those conditions and initiate discussions with clients about establishing them.

CLARIFYING YOUR STANCE

The framework for sorting out a stance begins by acknowledging that most staff groups have used their technology to develop and sustain a particular management system. That system is characterized by concentrating the components of organizational power in the hands of senior management. The key components of organizational power include literacy about the business, exercise of choice, access to business resources, accountability for the business, and competence to manage the business. For years, most staff groups have had their expertise used to support a system that centralizes this power and keeps these key components exclusively in the hands of a few.

One of Information Systems's core competencies is the retrieval, manipulation, and redistribution of relevant business information. In doing its work, the Information Systems staff generates products and services; these information products may take the form of reports, graphs, or databases. Traditionally, such products and services have supported a management system that tends toward centralizing the components of power at the top of the organization.

If you have any doubts about this, just look at the way Information Systems groups tend to create databases. The process of creating formats for databases is telling. Almost everything currently done in Information Systems is put together to make sense of data at a level that is relevant to senior managers. The way this information is formatted makes it meaningful in the eyes of those who are highest in the organization.

Because the information is designed for them, and what's retrieved is decided by them, it's not a surprise that this leads to literacy at the top about what's happening throughout the organization. What about the rest of the organization? How literate are people about the business?

The Finance staff's core expertise is the creation of useful measures to ensure good business decisions. Decisions by whom? Traditionally, the way the measures are put together focuses on satisfying the needs and wants of those at the top. Since financial information is being formatted and presented in a way that makes it clear and useful to those at the top, you find choice and access to resources most concentrated at the top.

The Human Resources staff's core competence is organizing human beings within a work setting to maximize the potential for business success. Human Resources staff know how to group people, how to build job designs, how to differentiate responsibilities, how to make communication work, and how to resolve conflicts. Human Resources technology has traditionally been focused toward the senior people in the organization. The technology has been used to support the position that the top is the important part of the organization. For years, Human Resources has believed upper management is the group that needs the most development, the most consulting time, and the most attention. Since management has a more profound sense of accountability for the business than anyone else in the organization, that's where Human Resources pays the most attention both in giving service and in responding to wishes about how Human Resources expertise is used.

> *Distribution of the components of power is a key way to increase capacity in an organization, because it multiplies the number of people who can make exceptions and give a unique response to the customer.*

THE IMPORTANCE OF TAKING A STANCE

Establishing a point of view about how your expertise should be used is important if you're promising to build your client's business. Are you convinced that paying attention to top management is the best means for doing it? Or are you persuaded you have reached a limit to the capacity you can build through such an upward-focused service?

The business value of an upward focus is nearly exhausted. It's been done for years, and it's been done well. However, there is little more capacity to be built at the top. The more we continue to work primarily with the top, the less return we are going to see. Attention should be focused elsewhere. If organizations are going to give a unique response to customers and deal effectively with issues of profitability, quality, and cycle time, the place where competence has to be increased is throughout the rest of the organization. This is where the five components of organizational power are thinly distributed. Only through a wider distribution of the components of power—literacy, choice, accountability, competence, and resources—will organizations move toward increased business capacity.

Two stories make the point.

The Bus Driver and the Utility Worker

Not long ago I was speaking in Dayton, Ohio. At the end of the day I returned to the hotel I was staying at and boarded the courtesy bus to the airport along with a weary group of travelers. As we departed for our destination, the bus driver—whose name, according to the placard on the sun visor, was Phil—launched into a long monologue about the hotel. The litany that followed was a list of complaints about the management, the facility, the service, and any other aspect of the hotel's operation one could imagine. For a full thirty minutes, as we made our way through rush hour traffic, Phil went on and on about the injustice, incompetence, and exploitation the hotel visited upon employees and customers. It could have all been summed up with "This is a terrible place to work and a terrible place to stay. If you are smart you will never come back here."

Contrast this with the story I was privileged to hear at a utility company. A customer service technician named Paul arrived at a customer's home to respond to an emergency call. When he announced himself, the customer proclaimed with substantial irritation, "I called you people hours ago. A valve on the hot water heater blew, the one you sold me and guaranteed! The basement flooded. I was waiting hours. I finally called a private contractor. He came immediately, fixed it, and charged me plenty. He wanted cash right now and I had to pay him. I can't afford that kind of thing. What's wrong with you people? Why can't you get here when there is an emergency?"

Paul didn't walk away, didn't start to argue, didn't blame someone else. Instead he said, "You are *my* customer and I blew it. I should have gotten here much earlier. I apologize and hope you will give me another chance. For now, why don't you let me look at the work that was done to make sure it is OK."

After he had inspected it he met with the customer, informing her, "The work looks fine. You may not know it, but we are responsible for reimbursing customers for this kind of work when we don't get here. If you will give me the invoice I'll reimburse you out of my own pocket and let the company reimburse me. I also want to show you where the master cut-off valve is in case something like this happens again. At least that will allow you to stop the flooding from getting out of hand. And finally I want to leave my name and number in case you have any further problems. Call me. I promise I will get back to you as fast as I can." The customer gave him the invoice. He paid it out of his own pocket, left his name and number, and departed.

Which company do you think will succeed in the long run? Phil and Paul are workers on the front line. To the customer they *are* the company. What accounts for the vast difference in how the two treated their customers? Paul was literate about the company, the business, and the risk it was at with customers in a deregulated world. The company had committed extensive resources to ensure that workers understood where the business stood. He exercised choice to create the unique response that the customer wanted in the moment. Most important of all, he chose to be accountable—to be the company to the customer. All this, the company supported. He is a product of a management system that distributes literacy and accountability throughout the organization.

Phil, on the other hand, was not the voice of the business whose bus he drove and did not see himself as accountable for that business. I doubt if he possessed much literacy about the state of the business or much choice in giving service to customers. In his mind, as in the minds of his managers, he had a menial job of little consequence. He was an employee to be controlled and held accountable, someone from whom compliance was expected. He was the product of a management system that consolidates literacy and accountability at the top.

Paul's response, by contrast, embodies the notion of increased organizational competence. It was a consequence of distributing power at the utility company—choice, literacy, accountability, competence, and access to resources.

A Major Role for Staff

The distribution process is profoundly affected by how staff groups work with line units and their point of view about the use of their expertise. Until staff groups are willing to change their focus and move toward wider distribution of power, increased capacity is not likely to develop. Business literacy cannot be widely distributed unless staff groups, particularly Information Systems, start using their expertise to distribute literacy throughout the entire organization. How will workers become informed about the financial impact of their decisions on the organization unless Finance groups create measures and reports that are useful and intelligible at the local level? Only then can workers make informed decisions about what's good for the larger business. As long as Human Resources staff groups don't widely distribute the competence for organizing and managing throughout the organization, how is the organization going to move toward increased capacity?

The participation of staff in the distributive process is essential. It is done in the service of building capacity.

A Business Position

Staff groups not only have to master a technology and be able to articulate it in business terms, they must also take a business position on how their technology will be used if it's going to have a positive impact.

It is irresponsible to say, "I don't care how the technology is used. I don't care how the theories and methods are employed. That's up to the client." It's irresponsible because it fails to choose accountability to the organization for business outcomes. The truth is it *does* make a difference how expertise is used. Simply to claim that how you're used is a client decision and exempt yourself from accountability is to choose not to be accountable for your impact on business results.

To take this seriously creates difficult issues. In meeting with clients, if I'm particularly preoccupied about my financial safety and security, I may find it troublesome to raise issues about the use of my technology. Clients may respond poorly to my point of view or find it inappropriate even to discuss my position. Perhaps the clients feel they have the right, the knowledge, and the authority to decide how my technology is to be used in their organization. They will not understand why I'm taking such a strong position about the matter. Any of these potential reservations encourage a cautious, muted response. Some examples follow.

TAKING A STAND AS A CONSULTANT

I was recently contacted by a major corporation in the Northeast that was struggling through painful changes. A two-day presentation to about twenty managers was scheduled to see if future work together was possible.

During the meeting we talked about their issues, trying to find some common ground for collaboration. The critical moment came in the early afternoon of the second day. I was discussing how I would approach the issues. I argued for focusing on the whole of the organization. They argued for focusing on the senior group and their problems working with one another. We were having a hard time finding common ground.

After a lengthy discussion, the management group wanted to deliberate on its own and asked me to leave the room. For an hour and a half I waited.

Finally, the managers called me back. One of them had been appointed spokesperson. He said, "We're not interested in this whole system approach. We don't think it's the time for you to be working throughout the organization. What we're interested in is team building and working better as a group. We, as leaders, have to become more functional and better able to deal with each other about the crucial decisions that we face. If you're interested in this work we would like to work with you, but we're not enthusiastic about your moving further down into the organization, working with union members, core workers, and line supervisors. We think the real issue is *us*."

Did I have the skills to do team building? Yes. Was I capable of helping them find some common themes and commitments as a group? Yes. I could have used expertise about how to deal with issues of conflict, accountability, and direction, and applied it to this group. I could have gotten the contract.

As I stood in the room at that moment, I felt the same old disappointing experience all over again. It would be one more contract to train senior management, a group that had already been worked with by many other consultants. I had no faith such a plan was going to resolve their problems or produce prosperity. I had no faith *at all* that this group by itself, no matter how effective they became in dealing with each other, would resolve the very difficult problems the organization faced: cynicism among employees, declining sales numbers, declining market share, and very tough union negotiations. I had no faith that simply doing team building with this senior group would increase the organization's capacity to surmount these problems and improve business results.

If I was committed to achieving business results, taking the contract under their conditions would have constituted a fraud. In essence, I would have been saying to them, "I believe doing team building with your top executives is going to improve business results throughout the organization." I did not believe it.

I replied, "I don't have any confidence that just doing team building with your group is going to resolve any of the difficult issues you are facing. You urgently need to build competence throughout the organization, and team-building workshops for a handful of executives is not an effective means to do it. The way to get positive change is not by continuing to pay attention to yourselves. It is a poor use of my expertise. The way to move things is to focus on enabling the entire organization so that every employee can act in service of your customers and the business. I think I would do you disservice if I took your time and money to simply focus attention on you."

The atmosphere grew rather grim. It was not what they expected or wanted to hear. They were saying, "We want to use your technology in the way we choose," and I was saying, "If you use my technology in that way, we will all be disappointed."

A shortsighted view would have urged agreement with their request. If I had been interested only in getting the contract, I would have acquiesced. But I knew mutual disappointment would be the outcome. I also knew that future business cannot be built on a foundation of disappointed clients. My no served their business and my business even though it felt unsafe and risky.

In the end, we negotiated with each other, finally agreeing on a scope of activities that satisfied both our agendas. They allowed me, with their support, to begin work with the larger organization. In turn, I agreed to do team-building work with them.

ANOTHER NEWSPAPER: TAKING A STAND AS A STAFF TEAM

A corporate staff team—Finance, Human Resources, and Information Systems—was asked to work at a major newspaper publishing subsidiary. It was facing an array of problems including declining revenue, dwindling market share, and low morale throughout the employee population. The staff team met with the management of the subsidiary several times to talk about the possibility of working together.

The initial sessions went well.

In the short term, the paper faced a multimillion-dollar cost reduction that needed to be carried out within three months. The staff team suggested that informing the entire employee population about the extent of the problem might be a good first step. It also described some methods for doing that so as to take advantage of the team's combined areas of expertise.

To the senior management members of the subsidiary, such a proposal was unthinkable. It contradicted every instinct they had. They wanted to put an optimistic spin on things, to smooth over the sticky issues, to be anything but explicit about the extent of the problem. They were willing to use any language but specific dollar language. They were willing to talk about the business having "a difficult financial problem" or "serious cost reductions," but they weren't willing to name the exact number.

It was a difficult meeting. The corporate staff team continued to explain its position. Kathy, the team coordinator, said, "Distributing literacy is the strategy we believe will make a difference. We don't believe it will do anything but undermine the organization to secretly huddle for weeks with us and yourselves to plan a strategy for cost cutting and then announce that decision to the entire organization three months from now. It won't build the organization's capacity to deal with the crisis. It will feed cynicism in people and support helplessness."

Finally the teams came to the agreement that they would announce to the organization the real extent of the company's financial problem in very specific terms. Management would disclose the specific numbers. Somewhat reluctantly, they agreed to work with corporate staff in carrying out the effort.

The following Monday, after the corporate staff team had left, management invited an external consultant to talk about the same issues. This particular consultant's area of specialty was strategic planning and visioning. During the discussion, management told the consultant of the plans to explain the problem to all the employees with the help of corporate staff. The consultant went ballistic. He insisted, "This would be a horrible error on your part. Your employees aren't ready for it. They don't understand the business issues. Emotionally, they will not be able to handle it. You are going to blow this place up."

In ten minutes, this consultant was able to reverse the decision. He had reaffirmed and validated all of management's original fears and reservations.

Kathy got a phone call to notify her of their change in plans. "We're not going to do what we decided in the meeting last week," Pete, the publisher, informed Kathy. "We still want to work with your team, but we don't want to announce the specifics of this cut. We think it's better that you consult directly with us as a senior group and let us struggle with these new ideas before we start to do anything radical in the ranks," he concluded.

The critical moment occurred later on that week, when Kathy flew down to talk to them about their change of plans. She said, "Look, our expertise, our technology, if it is to be used in a way that will make a difference, requires a willingness to distribute business literacy. We understand if you don't want to do that, but we can't promise to bring any value to your organization if you are unwilling to go in this direction. We don't believe we will serve you well by having another senior management meeting where we talk about these ideas and again focus on the group at the top. We think the only way that you are going to deal with these issues well is to engage the entire organization and make them knowledgeable about the state of the business. Literacy is the foundation of our approach to working with organizations. If we can't get agreement on that, we doubt we have much to offer you."

It was a very difficult moment. In the end Pete said, "We're going to do it. We're going to tell everybody."

What is the point? The situation forced the corporate staff members to come to terms with their beliefs about their expertise and its use. They had to take a stance! If they had acquiesced to the conditions, their presence would have had little or no impact on the organization. The *appropriate use of their technology* was the key issue Kathy had to negotiate with Pete.

If Kathy had not chosen accountability for impact, she would have said, "Fine, don't tell them. We'll work with you within the constraints you have described. We'll educate you about our approach. You're not ready to take this to the organization yet." In doing so she would have colluded with Pete and she wouldn't have been honest with herself. Being honest with herself meant acknowledging that to work only with a senior group wasn't going to take the subsidiary anywhere.

Management did proceed to inform the entire organization about the extent of the problem and, rather than the chaotic response they feared and the other consultant had predicted, they got a serious and sober reaction from the employees. The real surprise came when people thanked upper management for telling them the truth, saying, "This has never happened before. At least now we know what's going on. We feel you're taking us seriously."

The employees were no longer a group of anxious people without the capacity to deal with information. They were a group of anxious people who now understood what the difficult issue was, who wanted to be engaged in resolving the problem, who were thankful for having been told the truth, and who could manage their own fears and anxiety.

Kathy and the corporate staff team had bet the family farm in the interest of service and accountability. Pete and the entire subsidiary were deeply thankful for the risk Kathy and the team took.

INSURANCE FINANCE: CONSIDERING A STANCE

From the point of view of the Finance staff at the major insurance company mentioned in Chapter One, it was continually being besieged by requests from senior management for more reports, more data collection, more financial analysis. To obtain this data, the Finance staff went to the offices where the insurance transactions were actually occurring. They were the primary source for the information. The Finance group repeatedly made demands upon these work groups to collect information so that it could compile the reports.

The reports were irrelevant to the work groups themselves. They might be useful in answering questions senior management had, but to the work groups they were a waste of time. They felt powerless to stop intrusions by Finance. After all, Finance was the agent of senior management.

The process was predictable. Managers in New York City would deliberate about the cycle time of a work process or the educational level of employees at an insurance office in New Jersey. Because the managers at headquarters saw themselves as responsible for managing everything, they demanded more and more reports so they could be informed about the people and processes they were managing.

During a typical meeting, one of the senior managers might raise a question like "What are the trends over the last couple of years in large group business in the manufacturing sector?" or "How long is it taking claims adjusters in our New Jersey office to do a certain work process?" or "What are the demographics of our working population in the Westfield office?" It was easy to generate an unending list of requests for information.

These requests would invariably set the Finance group in motion. Often, the request was just an unexamined whim on the part of an executive, or a query raised by someone in the meeting without any demand that it be researched. The Finance staff, committed to a traditional posture, believed it must do whatever management even implied it should do.

One of the members of Finance began asking whether the group was convinced that creating all these various reports was building capacity in the organization. Some acknowledged it was not. Considering the time and energy drain on all concerned, it was *diminishing* capacity, especially in the work groups whose attention was being taken away from customers to retrieve data.

The fundamental question it raised for the Finance group was "Do we think we are increasing the company's potential to be successful by continuing to demand reports for the people *watching* the work from the people *doing* the work? Do we really think these reports will enable this organization to be more successful?" They concluded it was not the best use of their expertise.

They then had to ask whether it was a better use of their technology to construct reports for senior managers—or to construct useful measures for people in the working groups. Did the company gain more from better-informed managers or from workers who could improve the way they carried out their work process and the way they interacted with customers? They agreed that it made sense to provide useful tools to the work units, but they were reluctant to take a position that confronted the New York executives.

All this discussion finally led to a meeting between the Finance group and the work teams in New Jersey. Shortly after the meeting began, a member of a work team stated, "The way you're working with us, asking us to gather data so you can provide reports to senior managers in New York City, is not useful. You know that as well as we do. We want you to change how you work with us so we get financial information from you that will help us. What you are doing now has the opposite effect."

Unfortunately, I have no major success story to report. The Finance group did not disagree with what the workers were saying, but would not take a confrontational position with senior management. There was just too much risk.

In the long term a day of reckoning will come. In the end businesses will not tolerate groups or practices that diminish their ability to succeed in the marketplace.

THE SEWING LINE CASE STUDY

A clothing manufacturing unit in Texas provides another example of taking a stand. One of the core competencies of Information Systems is to retrieve, manipulate, and redistribute information to create business literacy. The Information Systems staff at all company locations was asked by the industrial engineers at headquarters to construct a system that would better monitor sewing machine operators at the plants. The goal was to build a tool that would tell plant management how any one operator was doing on any given day or any given hour, by specifying the number of operations completed and the quality of those operations.

The system was designed and tested. Information Systems was ready to implement. Orientation meetings were held throughout the plants to explain the system to operators.

One of the plants that would be involved was experimenting with self-managing sewing teams. A member of one of the teams objected to the system and raised a question with the Systems staff during orientation. "Do you really believe that one more system that watches us is going to increase productivity?

Couldn't you use your skills to help us become more aware of the business? Couldn't you put together a program to give us information that would allow us to make better decisions about the production we have to put out every day? From our point of view, monitoring us is not a good use of your technology if you want to help us move production."

For years Information Systems had used its technology to monitor, audit, and watch. The Information Systems staff in this facility had never before been confronted about using its technology to distribute literacy and choice to core workers. The sewing machine operators were taking a stand on what would serve their business and asked the Information Systems staff to take a stand about how its technology would be used.

As a result of this meeting the staff members suspended the implementation of the monitoring system in this particular plant. In fact, they withdrew it. They were still unsure how to use their expertise to get the outcome the operators wanted, but were convinced that more monitoring missed the point of what the work groups needed. It was irrelevant to them. More watching was not going to make any productive difference in the output of the work groups. Information Systems staff was left with a dilemma: if monitoring is irrelevant, how do we use our technology to serve these operators?

Every example speaks to the same questions. How do we propose our expertise be used? Do we use it to further centralize organizational power, or to distribute it throughout work units? Which direction best serves the business?

Once accountability for impact on the business is chosen, the products and services currently offered must be examined. What if you have chosen a distributive stance and your products and services support the traditional historical position of centralizing power? How do you create products and services that serve the opposite purpose—the wider distribution of organizational power? The next section speaks to these issues.

Choosing to be a business at risk in the marketplace with current and future clients will decide your value based on keeping a promise. The promise will have, at its heart, a commitment to build the business. Using technology is the means for fulfilling the promise. If it is poorly applied, it will fail, and in the long run so will the staff business. Taking a stance on the use of expertise is a service to the client and to your business.

EXPERTISE AND THE CHOICE FOR A DISTRIBUTIVE STANCE

A choice for the distributive stance creates a number of difficult issues. When staff groups choosing for the distributive stance examine what they currently know how to do well—the reports they produce, the software they design, the workshops they conduct, the programs they manage—they may come to two uncomfortable conclusions:

- Many or some of the products and services currently offered aren't really relevant to building business capacity in this organization. No solid business argument connects these activities to business results.

- Many or some of the products and services currently offered are not designed to distribute power throughout the organization but to consolidate and centralize it at the top.

The way out of this apparent impasse is to recognize that each staff group or individual possesses a core expertise that lies beneath any specific product or service offered. Somebody, at some earlier time, gave form to the traditional products and services currently used by staff groups. The programs they created were based on some underlying knowledge or theory. What did they know that allowed them to move from theory to application? Their completed products were things like strategic planning, reengineering projects, team building, software design processes, and training modules. What was it that enabled them to build those products?

NUCLEAR BOMBS, WEED WHACKERS, AND CORE COMPETENCE

I first came across the concept of core competence while working at the National Lab System, where "core competence thinking" was being applied.

The lab had recently redesigned the organization and created four basic groups or divisions. The first dealt with nuclear weapons—how to build them and disarm them. The second dealt with issues of national energy policy, global pollution, and other areas of national interest besides nuclear weapons. The third focused on transferring laboratory technology to improve industrial products. The fourth was the *core competence* organization. The design idea was that the first three were transitory organizations. The permanent group was the one that focused on core competence. It would remain the source organization for expertise to produce the products the other three organizations used.

Honda Motors has very successfully applied similar thinking. At Honda there is a core competence group that develops technology to design and manufacture small engines. Small engine technology takes various forms in Honda's product line, everything from motorcycles to weed whackers. Each of these products, for the next ten or more years, will require a marketing, sales, and manufacturing organization. Eventually, their time will come and go. New product organizations will emerge as the market changes and new small engine technologies arise.

What does Honda see as most essential to Honda? Not the weed whacker or motorcycle that is selling today, but the core competence behind it. Honda has the best technology in small engine design. In the coming decades, it will continue to apply that technology to vehicles, tools, and appliances that haven't been thought of yet. The same is true of the National Lab System. In future years it will apply its highly sophisticated expertise to all kinds of national and global issues. The organization that markets and distributes that technology may undergo major changes but the focus on maintaining competence and developing further expertise will persist.

It isn't any different for staff organizations. Each staff group possesses a core technology. Staff people have generated products that were appropriate for their time. Now they need to ask themselves about the products and services that have to be available tomorrow. How do existing products and services need to be transformed to be relevant to the demands of the current and emerging marketplace?

> *To express your core competence you cannot simply list the things you do. There is no proof that any of these activities really build capacity in the business.*

Core technology is what is critical to the development and survival of staff functions. Current products and services are transitory.

DEFINING CORE COMPETENCE

Among the participants in a recent workshop I attended were people from Finance, Engineering, Information Systems, and Human Resources. They became deeply engaged in the subject of *core competence* and how it applied to staff groups.

Initially, when members of each staff group asked themselves, "What's our core technology?" they would answer by naming specific products and services they offered: succession planning, strategic planning, software integration, transaction automation.

After a lengthy discussion a member of the Human Resources group reflected, "Isn't our core competence in Human Resources *knowing how to bring human beings together in ways that maximize the chance of business success?*"

The Human Resources people nodded in agreement. "We never have formulated it in that way," they said, "but that's really what we should know how to do."

Finance summarized its discussion by identifying its core competence: *"It's knowing how to create useful financial measures that lead to sound business decisions."*

People from Information Systems concluded that one of their core competencies was "knowing how to *retrieve information, manipulate it, and distribute it, in a timely way, to create business literacy in the organization."* They also claimed core competence in areas such as automation.

GETTING TO THE ROOT OF THINGS

Strategic planning and team building are specific products or services. You can describe, outline, and give definition to them. They also have a history. "Team building" has taken shape over the last four decades. It issued from a deeper expertise—understanding how to bring human beings together in a work environment to maximize their potential for being successful.

What's required is to become conscious of the roots—the core competence from which specific products and services have been created.

If you accept the premise that staff expertise should be used to distribute business literacy, accountability, and the other components of power, staff products and services should contribute toward that end. It may mean that you will have to create, learn, explore, and express your expertise in different forms than currently exist. Budget planning, team building, strategic planning, process consultation, software development, quality circles, or succession planning are each specific expressions of an expertise created at different times to meet specific needs.

For staff persons to have a major impact in organizations today, they must learn to give form to their fundamental competence in a way that is consistent with their beliefs about building the capacity of an organization. In the distributive approach, consultants who do strategic planning or process consultation would not say to a client in an initial meeting, "I do strategic planning and process consultation." Rather, they would begin by stating their underlying expertise. "My expertise is in helping people work together to maximize their potential for business success. I use it to help a unit move toward a wider distribution of literacy, choice, and accountability. My belief is that this can significantly increase business results."

The point isn't to sell a product. It's to uncover opportunities to apply core technology. Current products and services may or may not be relevant to a given set of circumstances. The requirement is to ask ourselves in what form our core technology could have potential application in a specific situation to build capacity in a specific organization.

If we limit our offer to our current products or services, we are missing the point of service. We have to lay claim to and have confidence in a fundamental expertise that has the potential to take a thousand forms in service of the business.

THE SAME BASIC QUESTION

From a practical point of view the distributive stance requires asking specific questions.

For the Finance professional: If my core competence is creating useful business measures, how do I use that expertise to create products and services that support the distribution of business literacy, choice, accountability, and the other components of power?

For the Information Systems professional: If one of my core competencies is accessing, retrieving, manipulating, and distributing information, how do I use that competence to create products and services that support distribution of power?

It is the same basic question for every staff group that chooses the distributive stance. Here are the basic issues:

- *Identify the core competence.*
- *Choose a stance about the use of expertise.*
- *Create the business argument to support the stance.*
- *Develop relevant products and services.*

EXPERTISE, PRODUCTS, AND SERVICES RADICALLY REDEFINED

All this may sound too theoretical. How does it work in practice? Three Human Resources staff groups recently went through the agony of redefining their expertise, products, and services after they chose to take a distributive stance regarding the use of their skills. The product of that work is the document that follows. For all the groups the task required forsaking products and services with which they were familiar because those products and services worked against their stance about the use of their expertise—distributing power and capacity to build the business. Their decision required they define their core competence and translate it into new products and services that were consistent with their stance. It has been difficult work.

DEFINITION OF HR CORE COMPETENCE

The following is a definition of the knowledge and skills [COMPE-TENCIES] that will be essential to Human Resources in the future if it is to create a credible and useful contribution. It is based on the assertion that in the end, after all is said and done, staff units will only survive when they are able to demonstrate positive impact on the issues their clients cares deeply about. In short this means that Human Resources will have to show how what they know and do improves the capacity of their customer units to do better. In practical terms this means: be more profitable, better the quality of products and services, shorten cycle times, and give an ever more unique response in the marketplace. Human Resources may only lay claim to continued legitimacy when they possess expertise and technologies that results in positively impacting the outcomes cited. Further, that expertise must be of sufficient complexity or changing so rapidly that it cannot be easily mastered or sustained by the customer groups they serve.

Human Resources believes that its expertise will have maximum impact on the results clients care about if it is used to distribute power and capacity throughout the client unit. This means creating and offering products and services to clients that broaden and deepen business literacy, access to resources, choice, competence, and accountability throughout the client's business.

The question becomes, "What are those technologies or competencies which Human Resources lays claim to or which they may learn that have such depth and the potential for such a powerful impact?" That is the question this effort is intended to answer. There are three families of competencies essential to fulfilling the requirements cited above:

- Competencies that enable a HR Unit to deliver its expertise or technology in a way that builds organization capacity.
- Competencies that build the capacity of the organization to fulfill its promise to its banker and customers.
- Competencies that build the capacity of the individual to contribute to the success of the organization.

COMPETENCIES TO DELIVER HR EXPERTISE

How to define the HR unit as a business at risk in the marketplace as opposed to a functional silo.

How to create an offer to the business units that makes a promise to increase the capacity of the unit to survive and prosper.

How to be clear, compelling, and credible in making HR expertise relevant and timely to the business needs of the organization.

How to enter the contracting meeting when the meeting is staff initiated, client initiated, or under a mandate established by others.

How to contract for agreement on the conditions essential to assess relevance, timeliness, and fit. Asking for and getting an agreement for the right and responsibility for an independent point of view. Contracting to raise difficult issues and to getting access to the necessary data.

How to create and give solid business reasons for your wants.

How to deal with resistance. Knowing how to process the meeting when things get really sticky and knowing how to raise the possibility of not proceeding with good will.

How to build and use a diagnostic model that will answer questions about issues of relevance, timeliness, and fit between the client unit and staff expertise.

How to discriminate between issues of fit and relevance.

How to take a participant-observer role in gathering data.

How to present feedback in a manner that raises the core issues about fit, relevance, and timeliness of using staff technology within the client's unit.

How to focus on the right discussion with the client, discriminating between a discussion about the relevance of staff expertise to the client's unit as opposed to a fit issue where the conditions to support the use of the expertise do not exist.

How to craft recommendations and move toward client ownership of actions to be taken.

How to process a feedback meeting gone bad and initiate a discussion of not proceeding with good will.

How to fashion a promise for application of your expertise collaboratively with your client.

How to identify, source, and choose the best scope and form of intervention discriminating between the pluses and minuses of training, consulting, individual, small group and large group models.

COMPETENCIES TO BUILD BUSINESS UNIT CAPACITY

How to "Lay Out the Playing Field" and answer the critical questions about the unit boundary, banker, and customer.

How to make every point of contact the customer has with the unit positive, understanding, and responsive.

How to create the language to make the offer to the customer in ways that are clear, compelling, and credible.

How to create business literacy throughout the unit.

How to offer the "New Contract" to unit members in a way that emphasizes mutual responsibility for the welfare of the business and new "membership requirements" for the future.

How to manage issues of conflict, dependency, self-interest, and purpose within the unit and change the conversations in support of accountability, action, and service to the business.

How to create structures within the unit that emphasize customer service over control and consistency.

How to construct business processes and deliberations that maximize the ability of the unit to deliver on its promises to the customer and the banker.

How to create job designs within the unit that maximize the opportunity for individual contribution, accountability, and new learning while fulfilling the business needs of the organization.

How to identify management practices and evaluate their impact on building the capacity of the unit to succeed in the marketplace.

How to redesign and invent management practices that support a culture focused on increased capacity, partnership for success of the business, and individual as well as unit accountability.

How to invent the better alternative to traditional management practices like performance review, management training, meetings, succession planning, career development and quality control.

How to reintegrate the managing and the doing in a way that minimizes the role of "watching" in favor of "doing" and services to the business.

How to eliminate expensive and time-consuming management tasks that add little if anything to the creation, production, sales, or distribution of products and services.

How to negotiate agreements with staff groups that focus on the needs of the business unit rather than the needs of the staff function.

How to get exceptions to staff and management demands for consistency when it is in the interest of the unit's business.

How to design reward systems that emphasize unit success or failure in the marketplace, the building of individual capacity, and mutual responsibility and accountability among all unit members for the welfare of the business.

How to create conditions within the unit that encourage the development of new knowledge and passion for the business among all unit members.

How to build self-sufficiency within the unit to continually diagnose and take action in the face of changing demands from customers, the banker or any key constituency that impacts its operations.

COMPETENCIES TO BUILD INDIVIDUAL CAPACITY

How to define, for the individual, choices about participating in the unit and taking personal responsibility and accountability for the choice made.

How to create, within the individual, value-based purpose and meaning in work and bring heart, hands, and mind into the workplace.

How to deal with loss of hope, helplessness, conflict, and disengagement.

How to define and understand what changes are required by the "New Contract" and translate those into individual terms.

How to become fully informed about the business of the organization and participate in creating a process that sustains that literacy.

How, as an individual, to deal with the politics of the unit and participate with integrity.

How to learn new competencies required for the business to succeed.

How to teach new competencies required for the business to succeed.

IN CONCLUSION

Perhaps the most radical idea in this book is the notion of staff groups choosing a stance regarding the application of their expertise. It seems to run counter to every notion of delighting the customer. It is not an idea that is embraced easily. While I can fully understand the reservations that are voiced in response to taking a stance, my experience leads me to the opposite conclusion: taking a position about the use of staff expertise is a deep act of service to the client. To knowingly apply expertise in a manner that will achieve limited results or do harm just because clients wish to do things their own way serves no purpose but to waste resources and, in the end, call staff competence into question. Pleasing and delighting are not service; improving results and building capacity are!

The issue of customer service often masks another even more knotty issue. What is the expertise staff groups lay claim to and how does applying it affect business results? A close examination of staff expertise may result in doubt and questions. Although we do them well, do our programs, practices, and procedures really make a difference? What is the business argument that supports their use? What are we going to do if we conclude that what we have been doing is obsolete and works against the stance we want to choose? To give up what we as staff do well is an act of courage. It makes us vulnerable, as June, the newspaper's manager of Human Resources, learned the hard way. It requires us to go back to the roots of our expertise and to invent, create, and modify programs and processes that are consistent with our intention and about which we are willing to make a promise and guarantee. Hard work. Difficult stuff.

I argue throughout this book that the most powerful use of staff expertise distributes business literacy, choice, access to resources, competence, and accountability. Other stances are certainly legitimate and have their supporting arguments. Whatever the stance chosen about the use of expertise, it is still the responsibility of staff groups to tell clients about it and to make the supporting business argument. It is also the responsibility of staff groups to offer promises and guarantees, no matter what stance they choose.

CHAPTER 5

OPTIMISM, HOPE, AND GOOD WILL

All this talk of being at risk, making promises, issuing guarantees, and taking a stance is potentially grim. It would be easy to see the foregoing as a call to try harder, sacrifice more, or redouble your efforts. What's new in that? It's the same old, same old. It could sound *deadly* serious and almost painful in spirit. Nothing could be further from what I intend.

Remember Judy, my wife, from the Introduction. She didn't want *just* my commitment. She wanted my optimism as well. They were both necessary. One without the other made no sense. Commitment without optimism would have invited my self-righteous suffering; it would have become heavy, tedious, and lifeless. In the end it would have burdened both of us. It was not enough. Judy demanded that I bring commitment *with* optimism and hope about what would be possible.

The choice for passion at work presents the same issues. The choice must be made with hope, optimism, and good will. If you are being dragged along or dragging yourself along, don't go.

What does it mean to *choose* hope, optimism, and good will? It means to embrace the excitement and anxiety of putting yourself on the line and offering something *you* believe will make a difference. It means choosing and creating a life in which *you* can believe. It means forsaking the wish that others can or will provide for your safety if only you can find a way to please them. It means forsaking all the experience that justifies being the cynic, the victim, or the bystander. It means choosing courage over security. It means doing all this without barter or the promise of a return.

In the workshops I have led in the last few years there is at least one discussion that always comes up when these ideas are presented. It usually begins with someone saying, "I agree—but don't you need sponsorship for these ideas before you move ahead?" or "I love what we are talking about but will it sell with senior management?" or "I believe, but why should I risk my job, even if I think this is right?" So on and so on. Everyone, including me, is worried about the price they must pay to take this path.

Sponsorship is helpful but it is not the point. To see it as essential is to continue to wish that someone other than I will sponsor the life I want to live. It is to wish for passion with safety. It is to demand that someone else bring into being the conditions that create my hope, optimism, and good will. It doesn't work that way.

What almost always remains unexamined is the price you pay if you *don't* do what you believe in. The price is to look back on your life with bitterness and disappointment. Passion, optimism, and hope are not possible when you are doing something that is not your best, has no worth, and actually makes no difference. Where is there room for despair when you have lived a life in which you have taken a stance?

If what you have read to this point makes sense to you, there is no easy way. The conversation between that part of you that seeks safety and that part of you that seeks passion and contribution is eternal.

I don't want to leave my heart in the car when I go to work. I don't want to pretend and live in a world of cosmetic relationships. When I choose for passion in my work, I choose at the same time for hope, optimism, and good will. This is not a book about reengineering. There is a heart to this book. The heart is not in the mechanics, practical and necessary as they may be; it is in the choice for passion, for service.

APPLICATION: TRANSLATING INTENTION INTO CONVERSATIONS

Part II moves from theory to application—from the abstract to the concrete. Chapter Six focuses on the initial conversations in considering work with a client—the contracting phase of staff work. It traces the steps in an initial meeting and gives examples and explanations of the key issues in contracting. After the chapter, the second Practical Interlude covers the steps and key points to pay attention to in navigating the initial conversations with clients. Of course, life doesn't go in a straight line, and I doubt that any contracting meeting has ever followed lockstep the sequence presented here. However, a specific model is a useful learning tool and does point to important issues that must be dealt with in managing a client relationship.

Chapters Seven and Eight outline a discovery process that staff groups can use to test the relevance, timeliness, and fit of their expertise and the client's business. It is a process that assumes a staff group has chosen a distributive stance regarding the use of its expertise. The Practical Interlude following Chapter Seven provides tips for analyzing the social contract within an organization to assess its capacity for partnership, and the one following Chapter Eight gives a list of sample questions useful for analyzing management practices and business architecture.

Chapter Nine concentrates on the conversations that occur in the feedback meeting when the issues of relevance, timeliness, and fit are considered by the staff group and the clients. It is in this conversation that the decision to proceed or end the relationship is made. The chapter is laid out in the same manner as Chapter One, presenting a model followed by examples and explanations of key issues. After the chapter, the final Practical Interlude summarizes the key points to pay attention to in managing a feedback meeting to negotiate differences over fit.

Chapter Ten summarizes the major learning points made throughout the book.

CHAPTER 6

INTRODUCING RELEVANCE, TIMELINESS, AND FIT

The discussion to this point has raised questions and presented choices. What is the stance to take in a staff role? What is staff expertise and how does it influence business results? What do staff groups offer the client?

The traditional staff framework falls short of what is required to have impact, so the challenge is to reinvent the staff role. Choices must translate themselves into practical action. No matter how compelling or attractive a theory may be, if the theory has no practical application for the client, it is of no value.

THE PRACTICAL WORK

When you apply the principles outlined in this book, you inevitably find yourself involved in conversations. Staff do most of their work through talking, through conversations with clients. It is conversations that create the client's understanding and expectations.

The first major conversation comes up in the contracting phase of working with a client. Initial contact with a client usually occurs based on one of three events: the staff group initiates the relationship, the client makes a request of a staff group, or some powerful third party initiates and mandates a working relationship between a staff group and a client. As Table 1 indicates, with the exception of the opening steps, the three kinds of meetings are very similar. In each of these meetings, the staff group is striving toward an identical end: to create the opportunity to see if its expertise is relevant to the issues the client organization is facing. Also, no matter how the meeting is initiated, the first step is to prepare for it. The major issue in preparing is adopting a clear and explicit framework for managing the meeting. The initial conversations with a client are not, at their center, about therapy, prescription, or mandates.

PREPARATION

It is in the initial meetings that the structure of the consultant-client relationship is defined. Once established, it is slow to change. It is difficult to overstate the importance of the initial meeting.

Traditionally, staff groups have been preoccupied with whether they can get the client to sign up, buy in, or roll out their programs. Preoccupied with this issue, they give a great deal of attention to the quality of the relationship with the client. "Is it going to be a tense meeting?" we ask. "Is it going to be uncomfortable? Will the clients be resistant to the work that we are suggesting? Will the clients have low energy? How can we convince them to sign up?"

The focus on relationships can lead us to mistake form for substance. Maintaining positive feelings is often seen as the key issue with a client. Staff groups have created numerous tools and techniques to navigate these emotional issues and move successfully through contracting meetings with clients.

One of the techniques staff people have traditionally used to solicit client support is *caretaking*. A wide array of caretaking techniques are used to manage clients when tension arises. If substantial and difficult issues are on the table and a client is being troublesome or expressing reservations, a classic staff response is to shift into "processing the relationship."

For example, a staff person involved in a difficult meeting might say, "As I am listening to you, it seems as if you have some reservation about proceeding. Maybe you have some concern about feeling vulnerable?" In

CLIENT INITIATED	MANDATE INITIATED	STAFF INITIATED
Make personal contact	Make personal contact	Make personal contact
	Acknowledge the mandate	Acknowledge the initiation and make the offer to the client
	Ask for the clients' concerns and acknowledge them	Ask the clients what contribution they think you can make
Ask the clients for their view of the problem	Ask for clients' view of the meeting's purpose	
Extend understanding	Extend understanding	Extend understanding
Ask the clients for their wants	Ask the clients for their wants	Ask the clients for their wants
Tell the clients your wants • Freedom to develop your own viewpoint • Access to information in the unit • Freedom to raise difficult issues	Tell the clients your wants • Freedom to develop your own viewpoint • Access to information in the unit • Freedom to raise difficult issues	Tell the clients your wants • Freedom to develop your own viewpoint • Access to information in the unit • Freedom to raise difficult issues
Be prepared to give business reasons for your wants • Relevance • Timeliness • Fit	Be prepared to give business reasons for your wants • Relevance • Timeliness • Fit	Be prepared to give business reasons for your wants • Relevance • Timeliness • Fit
Come to an agreement on the wants	Come to an agreement on the wants	Come to an agreement on the wants
Acknowledge the client's contribution to the success of the meeting	Acknowledge the client's contribution to the success of the meeting	Acknowledge the client's contribution to the success of the meeting
Restate the agreements	Restate the agreements	Restate the agreements

Table 1.

The initial meeting.

that moment, the conversation shifts from the substance of what is being proposed to the client's feelings. The conversation moves into a therapeutic mode; the client is encouraged to express what he or she is feeling. The point is to take the tension out of the meeting. The hope is that listening, extending understanding, and accepting the client's feelings will soften the caution or reservations he or she may have.

Relationship management remains an important issue for any staff group. I don't want to minimize its importance. Control and vulnerability require attention. The skills required to manage these are essential to providing service. However, those skills alone do not provide service.

Prescription is an alternative posture in the face of client reservations. This approach strongly implies, "We know better." Past successes and the benefits are cited. This is not an offer. "This is really such good stuff, you ought to do it. We've applied this process successfully in all kinds of places. It provides value in every setting we've tried it in." The recent popularity of reengineering is an example of a strong prescriptive stance. It was frequently touted as a universal good. In the face of objections, the implied but rarely stated question is "Why are you being difficult about understanding and affirming the value of what we're presenting? What's wrong with you?"

Yet another approach is *obtaining a mandate* or sponsorship from senior management. Senior management is solicited to sponsor what staff plans to propose to a client. There is no possibility of a client's saying no once senior management is behind the plan.

> No matter what your management told you to do or what needs to be done, you cannot come into this meeting with management's viewpoint. If you do, you are simply another voice for senior management.

All these techniques spring from traditional service postures. They treat working with a client primarily as a relationship issue rather than an issue of substance requiring the staff group to promise improved business results.

The Substance of Initial Conversations

Choosing to be a business at risk and choosing for accountability to business results leads to a major change in the preparation for initial client meetings. The shift is from preoccupation with the relationship and getting buy-in to a focus on the substance of the offer.

The starting place focuses attention on what is known about the clients and their business unit, the staff's offer, its expertise, and how, in a generic way, it can influence business results. In other words, given the business these clients are in, what's the best way to translate technology into potential impact on business issues?

Language must be found that is relevant to the clients and makes clear the intention to improve the business results of their unit. Preparation is finding ways to talk in the clients' language about building capacity.

INTRODUCING RELEVANCE, TIMELINESS, AND FIT

In the initial meeting with a client, the staff group needs to raise two topics to find out whether it can provide useful service. The first topic introduces the concepts of relevance, timeliness, and fit; the second, the conditions for a successful assessment of these areas within the client unit.

In the initial conversation with a group of clients, I am not looking for them to agree to do any work with me. I am not looking for them to sign up for a program, adopt a particular intervention, or buy a particular service. The first meeting is not about selling anything. Its purpose is to work with a client to answer three questions: What, if any, contribution can staff make? Is this the right time for staff to be here? and Can we work together?

To answer these questions, the conversation should focus on the relevance, timeliness, and fit of staff technology to the clients' business.

Relevance refers to the potential of staff technology to improve the clients' business results. In initial conversations the relevance of the theories and methods that constitute staff expertise are unknown. Whether or not that expertise can have an impact is a question that needs to be answered. One of the areas to come to agreement with the clients about is the means by which the relevance of staff expertise can be tested.

Timeliness refers to the current capacity of the client unit to pay attention to a staff intervention. The client unit may be too busy, too distracted, or too directed toward other concerns right now to be able to use staff technology. It won't help either you or the client if you become one more intervention on a list that is already too long. Using a technology takes dedicated time and resources. The answer to the timeliness question is unknown in the initial meeting with a client.

Fit refers to the use of staff expertise within a client unit. It may well be that the way a staff group believes its technology should be used is quite different from the clients' notion of how it should be applied. The clients may want to use staff expertise to sustain traditional management systems that consolidate organizational power. The staff group may see that using its expertise toward that end will have little if any impact on building the business, if its position is that wider distribution of organizational power builds the capacity of the client unit to succeed as a business.

Before any decision about working together is made, it is critical to come to an agreement with the client about relevance, timeliness, and fit. To do this is to ensure that the resources, effort, and energy of both our staff and the client unit aren't employed toward a disappointing end.

CREATING THE CONDITIONS FOR DISCOVERY

It is important to come to agreement with the client about creating the conditions that will test relevance, timeliness, and fit. There must be agreement on creating the conditions required to access these areas. There are three essential conditions. Staff should develop an independent viewpoint of the unit and the relevance, timeliness, and fit of its expertise to the business. Second, there must be agreement that the staff will raise difficult questions with the client when necessary. Finally, that the staff must have access to any and all pertinent information.

To ask for an independent point of view is to raise control issues. Control is a sensitive and central concern of line managers. In many ways, keeping control is their most sacred responsibility. Implied in asking for an independent point of view is the possibility that the staff may see things differently from the client. Controlling how things are seen is critical to most managers; agreeing to legitimize other viewpoints does not come easily. Because of all this, many staff people will object, "I wouldn't talk about an independent viewpoint, particularly in an initial meeting. It might offend the clients. They may find it inappropriate, view it as adversarial. It is likely to create tension in the relationship. What I want to create is a feeling of comfort and trust."

My response is "How can I give the clients my best view of the contribution we can make unless I have a point of view about it?" If I have to adopt the clients' point of view, I do them a disservice. I might like to believe that accepting the clients' viewpoint unquestioningly is a means of building trust. Then all I have to do is ask the clients what the problem is, what needs to be done, and how they would like to use my expertise. The truth is such an approach compromises the relationship. I am likely to do things I know won't make a difference. I need to develop a viewpoint just to be able to give an informed answer about what I think our technology can do. To do less is irresponsible. Trust is more likely to be the product of telling the truth than creating comfort in the moment.

The second agreement I want to have with clients is that we both accept the responsibility for raising difficult issues, specifically, differences about relevance, timeliness, and fit. Once I have had a chance to further understand the organization, I will be ready to come back and talk with the clients about the possible applications of my expertise. We may disagree about the relevance of my technology. We may disagree regarding timeliness and we may have serious disagreements about fit issues.

These can be difficult conversations. They are substantive. The wish to raise difficult issues directly with a client is an act of service. It says, "I don't want to make emotional comfort the highest priority in this relationship. I want to choose for substance. If it creates tension, so what? Our disagreements can be useful. I prefer that we both choose for the tension, if it is necessary to have the right conversation."

Finally, I must reach agreement with the client about having access to all necessary information. This is an obvious request. If I am going to develop an independent viewpoint about the opportunities to apply expertise, it must be based on accurate information.

In the initial meeting, I'm not thinking about how to sell the clients, how to get them on board, or how to create comfort in the relationship. I am focused on the issues that need to be fully understood before we can have a discussion about how to proceed.

I approach the clients by saying, "I believe I have an expertise that can have an effect on business units and results.

Let's face it. You're asking the client to distribute power and control, as well as to eliminate caretaking and judging. If the client is feeling no tension at this point, then you're probably not being clear.

What I don't know is whether or not that is true in your specific circumstances."

If the client challenges the value of examining relevance, timeliness, and fit, I must be prepared to give the business arguments that support the position I am taking. I don't want clients to buy into something that would have no impact on their business. I don't want clients to implement a program with no promise of making a difference. I don't want clients adopting costly and time-consuming procedures that will end up in disappointment and lost credibility for both of us.

My stance means I intend to bring value to the business or to withdraw. It says, "I'm not here to sell something, I am here to test whether I can bring value to the business, and I understand that no may be the right answer." I will welcome the no rather than do everything I can do to avoid it. I put myself at risk. My approach is not to be safe and sell. My stance is to be at risk about being of value. The stance I take reflects my intention. The most important thing is to choose to be accountable, to bring value, and to accept, going in, that value is still an unknown and that no may be the best answer.

THE QUALITY OF THE RELATIONSHIP

In looking at any of these issues with a client I do not abdicate concern about the quality of the relationship. But I have redefined what it means to pay attention to the relationship. If we are trying to form a collaborative partnership around improving the unit's business capacity, to "pay attention to the relationship" means that I speak clearly about substantive issues. The substance—the expertise, the offer and promise, the choice to be accountable for business impact, and the conditions needed to assess the relevance, timeliness, and fit of expertise for this client—is what forms the basis of the relationship. Safety is not won in making a sale or managing the relationship. Safety lies in the *value of substance,* something that is relevant, timely, and suitable for the clients.

What does an initial conversation sound like from this position? It is not only about thinking differently, it's about having different conversations with the client. The following story provides an example of how a conversation might sound.

ANOTHER INSURANCE COMPANY CASE STUDY

I met with three senior managers of the Sales Division of an insurance company. The meeting started with the senior managers laying out the difficult issues they were dealing with: declining revenues from sales, poor customer retention, deeply embedded cynicism, and helplessness among employees. The results of a recent attitude survey were bleak. The last issue they brought up was the deteriorating relationship with their corporate owners. The managers expressed their own helplessness and frustration throughout the presentation. Then they looked at me as if to say, "There it is, what do you think we ought to do now? What can you do to help?"

What do I say at this point? Do I focus on the pain they are living through? Do I ask them to talk more about their feelings? Do I attempt to be reassuring? Do I sell them a product that's designed to turn it all around? Do I sympathize and collude with them in assigning blame? Do I go to the flip chart and begin listing the ideas they have about resolving the issues? Do I talk about past successes?

It is my turn. They have done their part. They've laid out what they are facing.

I said, "The truth is I don't know whether my group can help. Our products and services may be of no value in these circumstances. I don't know if it is the right time to work with you. Even if it were the right time and I thought we could help, I don't know if we could agree on how to approach the problems. I don't even know if I would agree with your definition of the key problems."

The place to start is to acknowledge all these truths.

One of the managers interrupted, "You have one strange sales approach. If you don't know, how are we supposed to know?"

Asking for patience on their part, I continued. "I am committed to work with clients where I can have real business impact. If we were to work together, I would owe you a promise and guarantee tied to results. In your case, that means making a difference in sales figures, customer retention, the morale of your employee population, or your relationship with your corporate owners. Because I insist that I make a promise to a client, I am cautious about offering quick solutions.

"I have a viewpoint about how to approach these kinds of issues. When I work with an organization, I concentrate on some very specific issues. Let me name a few of them so you have some feel for the approach. I focus on the distribution of business literacy and accountability in organizations.

"The point of view is that traditional top-down, mandated interventions don't offer much help in dealing with the kinds of issues you have presented. I am convinced that in many situations an overall strategy calls for a wider distribution of business literacy, accountability, and choice to bring about lasting change that affects business results. What I can provide is the technology to support that direction. That's what I am about. The strategy is very different from what someone else might propose to you for managing change and resolving these issues."

I was meeting with a group where, for years, power had been centralized in the hands of a few. These people saw themselves as keepers of business literacy, the makers of decisions, and the people most accountable for the organization.

They started to press me, asking, "What do you mean by 'literacy'? And what do you mean by 'distributing choice'? How in the world would those things make any difference in this organization?"

At that point, I outlined the business rationale. "Let me take you out of the insurance business and into the hotel business," I said. I then told them the story of the shuttle bus driver who volunteered to passengers how much he disliked working for his hotel and what a lousy place it was.

"What gets my attention about that story," I went on, "is that an employee of a business, someone who is actually interacting with customers all day long, takes this position about *his* business. His behavior does enormous damage to customer relations. The parallel in your business may be someone at a service desk getting complaints from customers. He probably takes calls like that all day long and may have the same attitude about his job that the bus driver had. He might be saying to customers, "It's no surprise. We never get it right and on time. You are the twentieth caller this morning. I don't know what is wrong with us. We just seem to get worse and worse."

Or imagine a case where the caller's request requires something extra. Suppose your employee would have to get up from his desk and walk to another place to get an answer to the customer's question. The guy might find it easier to enjoy the comfort of his desk with the attitude, "Who gives a damn? I'll tell the customer whatever I need to tell him to get him off the phone. Move on to the next phone call. It's not my problem."

I concluded, "Distribution of literacy and accountability helps people who touch customers have the conversation with them that you yourselves would have if you were in their place. To have that conversation requires that they choose to be accountable for the business, that they be literate about it, and that they be able to grant the exceptions the client wants in order to be satisfied. Right now, you are the only people in this organization who are in that position. That is very limited organizational capacity for this company."

I paused and asked for a reaction. One of them replied, "It seems to me we are getting a little mixed up in this conversation. We are the client and you are the consultant. We decide what needs to be done and you offer help in doing it. Sounds to me like you have already decided what has to happen. Besides that, I am not at all comfortable with some of your ideas. You want to put the inmates in charge of the asylum."

I responded, "What you are saying speaks right to the point I am trying to make. Yes, I do have a viewpoint about how my group's expertise is best used. The issue is not who is in control and calling the shots. The issue is to be straight with you about what we can do to change things and get some results. If I said to you, 'Tell me what you want us to do' and then quickly agreed to do it, I would be giving you poor service. The truth might be that what you wanted me to do would have little or no impact. I want business the same as anyone else, but I don't want business where both you and I are disappointed at the end of the road. That is why I am taking such a strong position. I don't want to pretend that no matter how I work with you it will bring about change. It does not mean I want to call all the shots. It does mean I don't want to misrepresent what we can contribute.

"As to your point about the asylum and the inmates, approaching change with this intention is different. Apart from whether or not it is the right approach is the question whether or not you and others in the organization can live with it. The answer may be no.

"We both need to find out for ourselves the answers to three questions: First, is my expertise relevant to you and this insurance company? That means, do I know something that can help here? Second, is it timely for me to be here? Third—and most difficult—does your position on how to approach change fit with mine? In this last question I am asking if you can support a strategy focused on distributing literacy, choice, and accountability throughout the organization. Right now, I don't know the answers to those three questions, and my guess is you don't know the answers to them either."

One of them asked, "How would you proceed? What would you do next?"

I replied, "First of all, I wouldn't proceed with doing anything about 'the problems' yet. I think we all need to be as straight as we can with each other about the issues of relevance, timeliness, and fit. I suggest that you sign up for a very short-term, limited piece of work that will give me a chance to get in here, take a look at the organization, and discover places where I might make a difference. I might find persons at the complaints desk who are like the one I described, and that would be a place where we could focus attention. Or I might find places where we could improve business in sales or any number of other places. On the other hand, I may find little or no opportunity. At this moment I don't know the answer.

"It will also give me the chance to see if there is any support for approaching change in the way that we advocate—the fit issue. It is not just a question of you being willing to let go. It is also a question of others in the organization being willing to forsake their cynicism and choose accountability for this business. After I have a chance to better understand all this, let's meet again. At that point, we'll both be ready to reach some conclusion about proceeding or not proceeding together."

They chose to proceed.

The point of the story is to focus attention on the critical conversations about relevance, timeliness, and fit. They are the heart of the initial contracting meeting.

In Conclusion

You must come to agreement with your clients about the conditions under which your relationship will operate. Both staff personnel and clients should give voice to an independent point of view about the relevance, timeliness, and fit of staff expertise to the clients' business. Each is accountable for raising difficult issues about proceeding. Each is going to have access to information. Staff groups are a business at risk in the marketplace; for them to make a promise to improve business results, they need to know whether or not their technology is relevant and timely, and whether it will fit. If they don't assess relevance, timeliness, and fit and they make a promise, they are in jeopardy of failure. If their intervention succeeds it's probably only by accident.

THE STEPS IN A MANDATED CONTRACTING MEETING

The following material outlines and explains the steps in a mandated contracting meeting. Very few things go as expected, but it is useful to have in mind a road map of what needs attention in the initial conversations with clients.

I am using the mandated meeting because it is frequently the most difficult to manage. The client- and staff-initiated meetings are for the most part identical, with the exception of the beginning steps. However, they tend to involve less constraint and instinctive resistance, which makes them easier on both sides.

STEP 1: MAKE PERSONAL CONTACT

A staff person with a commitment to service makes successful personal contact with a potential client by:

- Choosing for good will.
- Bringing energy and enthusiasm.
- Committing to the organization's success.
- Choosing to learn.

You don't know who or what is the problem in the unit; in fact, you don't yet know whether there is a problem.

You also don't know if the expertise you offer can be helpful here.

Don't take management's side and don't take the clients' side. You are here to see if you can be helpful to the business.

STEP 2: ACKNOWLEDGE THE MANDATE

This meeting has not been initiated by you or the client. Don't pretend otherwise. State simply, and in a neutral way, the circumstances that brought about the meeting.

STEP 3: ASK FOR AND ACKNOWLEDGE CLIENT CONCERNS

Ask for the client's reservations about the mandate, and acknowledge them. Don't try to dismiss them, allay them, or minimize them. Just acknowledge that they are present.

STEP 4: ASK CLIENT'S VIEW OF MEETING'S PURPOSE

Explicitly ask for the client's view of the purpose of the meeting. Listen to it and acknowledge it.

Your task in this step is to invite the client to express their view of the meeting, listen to them, and acknowledge their feelings, their perspective, and their expectations or lack of them.

"What is your view of why we are here today?"

"What do you want to accomplish today?"

"What is all this about from your viewpoint?"

"Do you have any hopes or reservations for this meeting?"

Remember:

- You do not have to agree with the client's viewpoint.
- You do not have to defend management's viewpoint.
- You do not have to give your opinion.

STEP 5: EXTEND UNDERSTANDING

Being understood is a rare experience for clients. When you extend understanding to your clients, you are doing something very powerful for the relationship.

Extending understanding is a step beyond acknowledging the clients' viewpoint.

Extending understanding does not necessarily include agreement. In fact, at this stage you have no basis for agreement or disagreement.

Extending understanding means to summarize the content and feeling of what the client says. Simply saying "I understand" is not enough. You show your understanding by restating—not responding to—what the client has said. Summarize the content and feelings of what the client has said.

Keep your restatements simple. Use short, direct sentences: "You have little hope for this meeting because of your past experience with staff sent in by upper management. It sounds as though you're ready for another disappointment. Is that right?"

When you restate the client's viewpoint, ask if you've got it right. Keep restating until each client acknowledges that he or she has been understood.

STEP 6: ASK CLIENTS WHAT THEY WANT FROM YOU

In this step ask what the client wants from you personally. It is the start of negotiating how you and the client will work together. In negotiating a working agreement you need to find out exactly what the client expects from you.

If the client does not freely voice their terms or wants, probe for them. The client probably has something in mind about how they want to proceed whether they say so or not.

The client may want to talk about what they want from the project. This is important information. Here are some typical client terms and conditions:

- Certain matters about which the client wants to be informed.
- Where and how information you collect will be reported.
- How decisions are to be made between the two sides.
- Limitations on you, such as budget, time, access to people and information, and so on.
- Limitations on client's time and involvement in the project.

STEP 7: TELL THE CLIENTS YOUR WANTS

As a consultant you have three terms essential to agreement and proceeding. You cannot assess the relevance, timeliness, and fit of your expertise unless you get agreement on these wants:

- Freedom to develop your own viewpoint
- Access to all pertinent people and information
- Freedom to raise difficult issues

To establish the freedom to develop your own viewpoint, you might say, for example: "There are things I need from you if my team and I are to use our expertise well. First, I would like to have the freedom to develop my own viewpoint about the situation here. How do you feel about that?"

To establish that you will need to talk to the client and to other people who may have information pertinent to the development of an independent viewpoint, you might say something along the lines of "I will want to speak to people in your unit. I will also need some more of your time to get additional information about your own perspective."

To establish the freedom to raise difficult issues, you need to prepare the client to discuss them if you discover them. For example: "I need to be able to raise the difficult issues with you. After I talk to people, I may come back with something you didn't expect."

STEP 8: GIVE BUSINESS REASONS FOR YOUR WANTS

You must be able to state the business reasons for your wants. Otherwise, they are frivolous.

Questions of relevance, timeliness, and fit are essential issues needing to be raised, and your three wants are crucial to answering the relevance, timeliness, and fit questions.

If clients ask you why you want what you are asking for, give direct, good-faith answers. Trust that the clients are asking in good faith. This is probably the first time the clients have ever heard these requests or that a staff person has been explicitly concerned about relevance, timeliness, and fit.

"Why am I asking for these three things? When I'm collecting information and interviewing people, I'll be asking myself, 'Does my expertise have relevance, timeliness, and fit for contributing to the success of this business?' "

When you seem to be getting resistance from the client during the meeting, the odds are you're probably not giving an answer that is clear and makes business sense to the client.

STEP 9: THE CLOSING

Come to agreement on your wants. Restate your three essential wants and ask directly for agreement.

Acknowledge the client's contribution to the success of the meeting. Identify what the client has contributed to make the meeting successful, and say it to them. You may have to reframe your idea of a successful meeting.

Restate the agreements. Before ending the meeting, make sure both of you agree on what you're going to do next—and by when. Restate your understanding of what the client is going to do and what you are going to do.

CHAPTER 7

DISCOVERING
THE
POSSIBILITIES

Relevance, timeliness, and fit are all important issues to discuss with clients—but as you come into the initial meeting, you have very little real basis to evaluate them. Discovery is the process that will let you develop an independent viewpoint and assess whether your expertise has relevance, timeliness, and fit in the present instance.

THE DISCOVERY MODEL

The Discovery Model shown in Figure 1 looks at three broad areas: the social contract, management practices, and organizational architecture. The information collected during discovery is preparation for the feedback meeting to be discussed in Chapter Nine. In a more traditional model of consulting this stage is normally called a *needs assessment* or a *diagnosis*. There are two problems in this traditional approach.

PROBLEM ONE: MOVING FROM WHAT IS TO WHAT COULD BE

Diagnosis normally asks three basic questions: What is the problem? What caused it? and What has to be done to fix it? When your intention is to build capacity, you need a basic change of focus from what you look at when you're diagnosing for problems.

From a distributive stance the point is to find opportunities to increase capacity, to move beyond that which is to that which *could be*. It's a broader view and a longer-range view than staff generally take. It's not just keeping current systems in place, whether it's a performance review, an information system, or a budget control system. Even when all systems are working well—even when people seem perfectly happy, satisfied, and content—the discovery process is looking beyond what is there now to see where expertise can be applied in a way that will improve the unit's capacity in the future. Attention focuses on what *could be*.

There is always opportunity to increase capacity within business units. The discovery phase is focusing on potential. The idea that staff groups are here to simply sustain or maintain the status quo, or that we

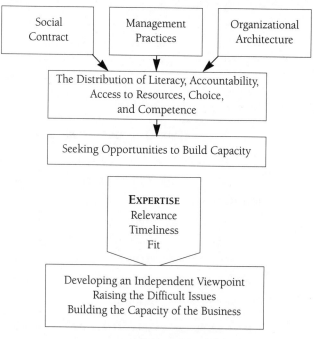

Figure 1.
The Discovery Model.

are here to do preventive maintenance or to fix things that are broken, seriously limits the contribution staff technology can make.

PROBLEM TWO: CHANGING WHAT YOU THINK IS IMPORTANT

The second problem is the hidden bias present in the older model. It influences how questions are asked, how information is gathered, and how sense is made of that information in forming a picture of a client unit.

Every staff group embraces an assumption about how its technology ought to be used. This assumption may be unexamined, unspoken, even unconscious, but it is still there. The hidden bias has direct impact on every aspect of a staff group's activities: how it defines itself, the purposes and goals it embraces, the interventions it proposes, and the relationships it forms with its clients.

This hidden bias is embedded in the staff group's beliefs about what ends its technology should serve. Traditionally, staff members take for granted that their expertise should promote the consolidation and centralization of power at the most senior levels of the organization. They are convinced this stance contributes to the welfare and survival of the larger institution. It is so deeply accepted as a premise for staff operations that it is generally unquestioned. It has serious impact on what staff groups pay attention to.

HUMAN RESOURCES AND FINANCE: PICKING A PURPOSE

As I mentioned earlier, I recently sat in on a meeting of Human Resources professionals at a very well-regarded organization. The focus of the discussion was on the future of the Human Resources Department, what it ought to become over the next three to five years. During the course of the discussion, members of the group were offering their own thoughts about the future role of Human Resources. One of the members spelled out his view: "My belief is that we ought to be developing those at the top to become the finest senior managers in the world through succession planning and management development. And we ought to be developing practices and policies to protect the corporation from the rest of the employees."

The wave of protest I expected from other members of the group failed to materialize. Although others might have stated this viewpoint in more politically correct language, there was no fundamental objection to the idea. "We are here to serve the top by increasing their competence, literacy, and ability to control the rest of the organization" is the traditional staff position. The attention is on leadership and control.

Other examples of the same traditional position come from the sewing plant in Texas and the insurance company in New Jersey. In both places, small business units within the larger organization were making a serious effort to take increased accountability for their own operations. They quickly discovered that they had a great need for specific financial information about their unit's operation in order to make good decisions. In both cases the groups asked the Finance function to work with them to create timely and relevant financial measures to meet their needs. In both cases the answer was no—and the reason for the no was the same. The response of Finance went something like this: "We don't have the time to construct such measures; they are at the bottom of our priority list. Our primary task is to satisfy senior management and their needs for information. In fact, you're mixed up about the relationship. We make requests of you for information; you don't request services from us!"

They might just as well have said, "We are here to build the literacy, competence, and range of choices that senior management has available. The senior managers are accountable for this business and we are a resource dedicated to them."

As has been pointed out earlier, this centralized power orientation has serious consequences to both the staff groups and the larger business. Leadership and the needs of leadership become all-important. Establishing and sustaining consistency throughout the organization demands attention. Contributing to the establishment and maintenance of control becomes a focal point for staff diagnosing and intervening in the business.

Holding the centralized power position leads to needs assessment that looks for problems so that breakdowns in the system can be repaired. The system itself is not questioned. From a distributive position, the intent is to discover ways to build capacity in a business. The focus moves from leadership, consistency, and control to the distribution of literacy, accountability, and the other components of power.

BUILDING CAPACITY

So what is meant by *building capacity?*

It means discovering opportunities to further distribute the components of organizational power—business literacy, accountability, choice, competence, and access to resources—throughout the organization or business. Full capacity is realized in a business unit when at every point of contact with customers, each unit member gives the best possible response. Beyond customer satisfaction, it means every member of the business unit is both enabled and eager to contribute to improved quality, shortened cycle time, and unit profitability.

Interviews at all levels and for all staff projects need to be done with the intent of building everyone's capacity. The goal is to find opportunities to ensure that at every moment the unit under study is offering and delivering uniquely appropriate responses to customers or other constituencies.

The discovery process focuses on answering this question. To accomplish this, staff looks at the current distribution of business literacy, accountability, choice, competence, and access to resources. If the staff group possesses technologies or methods that will contribute to broader and deeper distribution of these components of power, then it has areas of expertise that are relevant to the business. If what the staff observes in the discovery process—meetings, conversations, job designs, management practices, and such—is all working to serve consolidation and centralization of the components of power, it most likely has an issue of fit with its client. If during discovery staff finds that the unit is overwhelmed with demands or distracted by multiple concerns, it may have a timeliness problem with the client.

BUSINESS LITERACY

If the distribution of power is the means by which expertise builds capacity, staff groups start the discovery process by gathering information about the distribution of business literacy. How widely distributed in this business unit is knowledge about its critical measures? How profitable is it? Who are its customers? What is its offer to the customer? What are the constraints it has to operate under? The answers tell how widely distributed knowledge of the business is. The more widely distributed the business literacy, the greater the business capacity of the unit. If such business literacy is not widely distributed, it limits the opportunity for individual members of the unit to give the best possible response to a customer.

For staff gathering this information, questions start to form. "Do we have a technology that could increase and sustain the distribution of business literacy in this unit? Is there deeply embedded opposition to disbursing business literacy? Or is there indifference to becoming knowledgeable about the business?"

ACCOUNTABILITY

Another key category in the discovery process is *accountability*. Who chooses to be accountable for the success and welfare of the unit as a whole? Is it only those at the top who feel accountable? Or is accountability more widely felt? Attending meetings provides opportunity to get useful information about this issue.

THE NEWS SUBSIDIARY: ACCOUNTABILITY IN ACTION

Early in the work Kathy did with the newspaper, she had occasion to have all the senior managers in the room for several days. Many of them felt meeting as a senior management team was at best frustrating, and at worst a total waste of time. In the course of observing their deliberations it became apparent that the majority of the members had little if any interest in choosing to be accountable for the whole of the business. They limited their definition of accountability to their own department or function. Typically they showed little interest in any discussion that did not directly connect to their group. If the parent company was clearly dissatisfied with the financial performance of the paper, it was the publisher's problem *and the publisher's problem alone*. From this stance, of course, the meeting was a waste of time and irrelevant to the majority of participants. Given their perspective, who would want to be there? People who attended felt like hostages.

Imagine the difference if these managers could have entered the room saying, "I am as accountable for this institution as the publisher of this paper is. I care deeply that these meetings focus on relevant and pertinent issues concerning the welfare of the entire newspaper." Such an attitude would instantly multiply the capacity of the business.

The meeting provided valuable information about the organization. It enabled Kathy and the corporate staff team to ask themselves concrete questions about their potential relevance, the timeliness of their intervening in the business, and the fit they might achieve with this client.

The company actually published two separate daily newspapers, one aimed at in-depth treatment of news, the other featuring stories of more popular interest. One of the more troubling conversations during the meeting involved the editors of the two papers. Both saw themselves as disconnected from the rest of the business: advertising, circulation, and production. This detachment from the rest of the business was not accidental; it was treated as an issue of principle. For editors and reporters to take seriously the issues of circulation and advertising might compromise the integrity of their journalism. Yet circulation and advertising were highly dependent on the content and presentation of the newspapers to attract advertisers and readers. From a staff perspective Kathy had to ask herself, "Do we have methods or processes that can increase the felt accountability for the whole institution in this group without compromising values that are so dearly held? Is distribution of accountability for the whole business going to be opposed by this group as a matter of principle?"

In subsequent work, the editors of both papers came to terms with the larger responsibility. Rather than choose for accountability only to their own Newsroom, they each chose to be accountable for the entire institution. The moment they did that, it changed their attitude about being in those meetings.

Before they made that choice, they had no interest in talking to Circulation or Advertising. Their view was that Circulation's problems were Circulation's problems and Advertising's problems were Advertising's problems. Their only problems were the Newsroom's problems. Their job was to put a newspaper out. If Advertising couldn't sell ads and generate revenue and if Circulation couldn't sell the papers, it wasn't their concern.

Once they made the choice to be accountable for the success of the institution, they saw their role differently. They said, "Circulation *is* my problem just as much as it's the publisher's problem. Advertising's my problem, too, just as much as it's the head of Advertising's."

The result was to recognize that the Newsroom had to enter into conversations, commitments, and promises with Circulation and Advertising if they were going to live out a commitment to the institution. At the same time, the integrity of the journalism had to be guaranteed. It dramatically changed their relationships. It profoundly changed how the company operated.

Discovering how widely the choice for accountability is distributed in an organization requires looking beyond the senior level. The same questions must be asked throughout the entire organization.

Cynics, victims, and bystanders are important indicators of the distribution of accountability. *Cynics* are people who have no faith or optimism about the future, the company, or its management. *Victims* are people who feel that they are living in an abusive, difficult, conflicted environment and are helpless to do anything about it. *Bystanders* are just interested in watching what's going on; they don't see themselves as making any difference. The presence of cynics, victims, and bystanders indicates that people do not choose to be accountable for the institution. What all three groups share is the belief that someone else is responsible for making it all work.

It is not unusual in large organizations to find only one person who actually feels accountable for the entire institution. Many might feel accountable for something, but it is only for "doing my job" or "running my work unit" or "running my division."

If this is how narrowly accountability for the institution is distributed, how could any organization ever have a genuine opportunity to maximize its capacity?

COMPETENCE

A third area of focus is *competence*. Competence is all the skills necessary for a business to keep its promises to customers and bankers. It is what must be present in a business unit for it to make and deliver on its offer in the marketplace. To build organizational competence requires the development of individual competence. The more competence people can develop and master, the greater their individual capacity to contribute to the unit's capacity.

Inquiring about attitudes toward learning and teaching unearths a good deal of information about the distribution of competence. It means discovering the feelings toward learning new skills and the willingness to transfer skills to others. It is not unusual to find a negative attitude toward new learning, learning that would serve the organization and the individual business units. In some organizations, there are formal policies or procedures that restrict new learning. In some unionized organizations, job descriptions may seriously restrict the activities workers are allowed to perform. To do some task that belongs to another job would be a violation of union contract. It is common practice for training and education budgets to be cut when times are lean. It is commonplace for people to invent excuses to avoid attending a seminar or a training session.

When staff members look at the potential for relevance in the area of competence, they ask, "If we could distribute competence in a broader way, would this increase the capacity of the business unit to deal with its customers as well as its cost, quality, and cycle time problems? Do we have methods that would contribute to achieving this?" When considering fit, they ask, "Are people willing to learn new and unfamiliar skills? Are people willing to transfer and teach skills to others that they may have guarded jealously for years?"

IN CONCLUSION

It is crucial to seriously test the issues of relevance, timeliness, and fit before engaging in work with a client. To do this, you need to make explicit and take a stance about the use of your expertise in service of the client.

The social contract—the distribution of business literacy, accountability, choice, access to resources, and competence—is important in assessing relevance, timeliness, and fit, thus suggesting a framework for gathering information. The following chapter outlines additional dimensions of the discovery process.

PRACTICAL INTERLUDE

KEY POINTS IN THE SOCIAL CONTRACT

The social contract within an organization should be based on a clear, mutual understanding between the individual and the unit. Does a partnership or a parent-child relationship exist? To determine if a partnership exists, look at the management practices and the architecture of the organization. The questions to ask focus on the elements of partnership:

- *Is everyone fully informed?* The following points will serve as a checklist for business literacy. As you talk to people in the client unit, see what they know about each of the listed areas.

  The business mission

  The customer

  The unique value added for the customer

  The key results

  The constraints

  The difficult issues

  The dominant cultural principle: partnership or parent-child

To assess economic literacy, see how people regard the relevance of this information to their personal situation:

  Personal accountability

  Goals and objectives

  User or customer satisfaction with the business

- *Is the emotional contract clear and explicit?* That is, do people have real and felt personal responsibility:

  For personal motivation

  For optimism

  For commitment

  For the success of the organization

  For clarity about a personal sense of purpose

CHAPTER 8

FURTHER OPPORTUNITIES FOR DISCOVERY

Discovery is a deeper and more productive process than traditional staff needs-assessment and diagnostic procedures. As discussed in the previous chapter, the intent of discovery is to create maximum business capacity through a broader distribution of the components of power: business literacy, choice, accountability, competence, and access to resources. Only with such a distribution can the maximum competence of an organization be brought to bear upon each customer, supplier, and regulator, as well as profitability, quality, and cycle time.

The purpose of the discovery process is to come to terms with the questions of relevance, timeliness, and fit. Is your staff expertise relevant? Will it develop the unit's ability to build business capacity? Is it timely? Are the time and resources available to pay attention to the introduction of your expertise? Is there a fit? Does the unit take the same position as you do about the application of your expertise?

MANAGEMENT PRACTICES AND
ORGANIZATION ARCHITECTURE

To expand the discovery process, this chapter discusses how to look at an organization in two additional ways, from the viewpoint of its management practices and from the viewpoint of its organizational architecture.

Management practices are the formal and informal rules, policies, and procedures that govern, control, and coordinate the efforts and activities of all members. They include the dissemination of information, performance reviews, attitude surveys, hiring procedures, and deliberation processes.

Organizational architecture refers to the structures that give the organization definition. Although these structures are not permanent, they are very slow to change. They include how jobs are structured, how the organization is grouped, how staff departments operate, how the management role is defined, and how rewards are distributed.

Management practices and organizational architecture reflect assumptions regarding the distribution of organizational power. Frequently, practices and architecture work to consolidate and centralize power—and staff groups are frequently the creators and keepers of practices and architecture. Human Resources often controls hiring practices, performance reviews, job descriptions, and a host of other activities. Information Systems controls the practices that govern the distribution and formatting of critical business information. Finance controls the development of budgets, strategic planning processes, and control protocols. Engineering and Quality have considerable influence on the rules and practices that govern work processes. Staff groups reveal their stance about power in the practices, policies, and structures that govern how work gets done.

MANAGEMENT PRACTICES

It is useful to examine various management practices and policies to see whether they encourage the distribution of power or restrict it. One of the best indicators of power distribution is the pattern of information flow in an organization.

Numerous practices and rules govern the dissemination of information in almost all organizations. Particularly sensitive is information about difficult issues facing the organization: Are we off budget? Do we anticipate cost cutting in the near future? Many of the difficult issues being guarded are financial. Others are about new ventures being contemplated or variations in products or services. Restructuring issues are often kept confidential. Discussions about the possibility of outsourcing certain functions are cloaked in secrecy. Some managements are almost phobic about telling the rest of the organization the profit margins required by their bankers. Practices are created to restrict access to this kind of information. Passwords are required to get into computer programs, constraints on who can attend certain meetings are established, and the distribution of sensitive documents is closely monitored.

In an organization I recently worked with, telling employees the specific profit margin was prohibited. A manager could call it large or small, but could not name the specific number. It was privileged information. Great pains were taken to preserve secrecy, so much so that even in the senior group, when the CFO distributed handouts showing the number, the handouts had to be returned at the end of the session to ensure that no copies went out of the room. These kinds of practices tell you a great deal about an organization and are a testing ground for relevance, timeliness, and fit of your expertise and stance.

Practices that emphasize the differences between managers and workers can also be strong indicators of fit and relevance issues. Here are a few common and traditional practices: Managers give performance reviews; it's done top down with a parent-child flavor. Managers hire. Managers decide changes in work flows and business processes. Managers are the ones who interact with the customers, not workers. Such practices and policies usually restrict the distribution of literacy, choice, and resources. These practices make *management* a class of people rather than a set of tasks.

When assessing for relevance, timeliness, and fit, the issue is not whether information and management practices are being implemented as they were designed, but whether *they build and sustain maximum capacity.* If staff expertise was used to redesign these processes, could opportunity for

All these are questions to give you information about relevance, timeliness, and fit. Questions about the social contract usually bring up important fit issues in an organization.

building capacity be created beyond what that system is now capable of doing? Even if it's working the way it was intended to work, the current process may not represent maximum capacity.

ORGANIZATIONAL ARCHITECTURE

An organization's architecture—the structures that give it definition—is slow to change. It includes areas such as groupings, role and job definitions, and the design of compensation systems. Once again these areas are particularly relevant to staff groups because their role often includes designing and controlling these structures.

Staff technology or expertise takes form in the design of organization architecture. The discovery process can reveal the bias staff groups have embedded in the design of jobs, reward systems, and other structures. To find the bias, ask whether the job designs contribute to building maximum capacity in this business unit. Do the organizational groupings promote the distribution of literacy, competence, and accountability? Is the reward system encouraging the development of business literacy and the choice for accountability? Or are the groupings, job design, and reward systems supporting the consolidation of power by focusing on control and consistency?

Once these questions are answered, you can focus on relevance, timeliness, and fit. You can ask how these structures would look if they were intended to support the distribution of literacy, choice, competence, access to resources, and accountability. Other useful questions: Do we, as staff, have the technology to redesign these structures so that they have more potential to contribute to the success of the business? How much opposition is there in the client organization to change aimed in this direction?

GROUPINGS

Functional organizations frequently limit the quality and uniqueness of response to the customer. The customer is interested in the overall service of an organization. For instance, if I am a retailer doing business with a clothing manufacturer, I'm interested in getting the product I want, in the sizes I want, with the necessary merchandising material, on time. It is that simple. If I have a complex problem with an order that has just been delivered, I want to resolve it with one call to one person. If I have to deal with a functional organization divided into Sales, Manufacturing, Distribution, and Merchandising, there is no single source I can call to deal with the problem. I've got to go to Sales for the sales part of the problem, to Distribution for the delivery part, to Manufacturing for the wrong items part, and to Merchandising for the missing support materials. Many businesses make their customers jump through hoops like these.

During discovery, staff looks at how an organization is grouped and whether it's directed toward giving a unique response to the customer or toward keeping tight control of the operation.

WORK PROCESS AND JOB DESIGN

Examining work processes and job designs are part of the discovery process. Relevant questions: Do the work processes encourage new learning and teaching? Do they encourage the building of individual capacity by encouraging the acquiring of new competence and applying it? Do individuals view work narrowly as "their job" or more broadly as a set of tasks to which each individual contributes maximum capacity?

STAFF ROLE

The role staff plays in an organization gives a great deal of information about relevance and fit. Are staff groups responsible to operating units or are they responsible to senior management? Do they see their job as building capacity? Do they see their responsibility as maximizing the potential of the business units to survive and succeed in the marketplace? Do they have a positive impact on and choose to be accountable for the cost, quality, and marketplace issues of the business units?

REWARD SYSTEMS

And finally, take a close look at reward systems. What do reward systems reward? Is there any reward for becoming business literate or increasing competence? What are the built-in assumptions around reward systems? Do the compensation systems put everybody at risk based on performance? Do they try to promise safety? Do the reward systems reward units for their response to customers or for their compliance with internal policies and regulations? What's the method for distributing wealth? What's the difference between the lowest-paid member of the organization and the highest-paid? And what is the implication of that? Is the organization merely looking for cheap labor, or is it searching for employees willing to increase their competence, choose for accountability for the organization, and manage their job as well as do it? Which of these stances does the system reward?

THE SEWING LINE: SEARCHING FOR POSSIBILITIES

What follows is an example of working through the discovery process. The setting is once again the large manufacturing plant. The product is clothing—shirts and trousers. The workers are grouped in departments called lines, consisting of about a hundred operators each. The operators are organized in a long line, each sitting behind a sewing machine.

The work process starts with cut pieces of fabric at one end. The fabric passes through forty to sixty individual operations and emerges as a finished garment at the end of the line. Each operator is assigned one operation. For instance, one person puts the belt loops on a pair of pants, then passes the garment to the next operator. The next operator sews on the back pockets, then passes it on to the next operator. Each operator does one thing, then passes it on to the next operator. No operator has responsibility for more than one small step.

The more traditional staff view is interested in a limited number of questions: Are the operations lined up correctly? Is each of the operators doing the assigned operation correctly? Can we change the hand movements of these operators a bit to get a little more efficiency out of them? If all this is in place, I assume that this is maximum capacity for this group. If I do a diagnosis as an industrial engineer, it is with the intent to keep the line working as it has been designed. The commitment is to a work design that is based on control and consistency.

In contrast, seeking opportunities to build capacity looks beyond what is wrong with the detail of the current design. It asks whether this work configuration as a whole establishes maximum capacity for this manufacturing unit. Are there opportunities to distribute literacy, competence, and accountability in service of business results?

I was part of a team that started working with this plant as the manufacturer was expanding its product offerings. The manufacturing lines were being required to change their work process and operations so as to manufacture a broader product line. They could not keep manufacturing the same product year after year. When plants tried to introduce new product construction into these traditional lines, it took weeks to bring operators to an acceptable level of efficiency. New operations were difficult to learn, additional supervision was needed, and the training was very slow. There was endless complaining from operators about having to learn new skills and about all the changes.

When we saw how easily the line's results could be eroded by simply introducing a new product, we said to ourselves, "If we distributed competence, choice, and literacy, is it likelythat this action would result in a production line that could successfully change itself much more quickly?

DISTRIBUTING LITERACY

We wondered, "Would the operators be better able to learn, teach, and deal with change if they understood the business better?" Literacy in this case meant both business literacy and work process literacy. "What if workers knew plant after plant was closing, sending manufacturing offshore, because of lower wage costs and lower workers' compensation costs?"

The plant's competition was global. Management was greatly concerned about the ability of domestically owned and operated plants to reduce unit costs enough to be competitive with manufacturing costs in Mexico. Workers' compensation costs were increasing so rapidly in this plant that they had become the major factor in rising production costs. Repetitive motion injuries and other work-related problems were almost out of control. We asked ourselves, "Would it make any difference to business results if we distributed this information widely among operators?"

Another potentially important piece of literacy was work process knowledge, the steps that are required to make a pair of pants. Most operators simply knew their assigned task and handed the garment on to the next person. They didn't know what the overall construction process was.

If the operator who did a certain operation was out for the day, garments would pile up at that work station. There was no way to move garments through the rest of the line with the required efficiency. Half the line might end up doing nothing, while the other half was producing half-finished garments.

Even when fully staffed, the lines couldn't achieve balance or an even flow. Sewing machine operators worked at different rates of speed and the lines would frequently back up. Bottlenecks played havoc with production numbers and unit costs.

Would distributing literacy, competence, and choice make any difference in resolving these issues? What is the business argument that supports such action?

Distributing Competence and Choice

All these job design and work process issues were potentially germane to the distribution of competence and choice. Whenever a sewing machine broke down, an operator had to wait for a mechanic to come and fix it. There were a thousand operators and only six mechanics in this plant. As a consequence, operators were frequently sitting waiting for the next available mechanic to do something as simple as changing a broken needle. Only the mechanics had the authority to perform those tasks. The process of finding a mechanic was tedious and complex. It began with an operator having to tell a supervisor about the problem, who in turn had to tell a manager, who in turn had to tell the head mechanic, who in turn had to assign the task to the next free mechanic. It was not unusual for such a process to consume more than an hour before someone got to the ailing machine.

The primary role of supervisors seemed to be giving permission to operators to move from one work station to another. Supervisors also acted as intermediaries between operators and other staff within the plant.

It was the industrial engineer's job to look at a garment, break it into separate operations or pieces of construction, and then decide how an operator could do each of these operations with maximum efficiency and effectiveness.

In testing relevance we asked whether results would improve if operators mastered two or three operations. Would results improve if operators had the authority and skill to make simple repairs to their own machines? If they had the latitude to move about as necessary rather than waiting for permission? Would it make any difference if they were able to break a garment into a construction process and implement that process on their own?

All these questions are questions about relevance. Relevance requires us to ask, "Do the stances we bring—advocating a distributive strategy—and the technology we offer—methods to distribute literacy, competence, and the other components of power—have any application in these circumstances?" Additionally, it makes us examine where and how staff technology might be applied. "Where would we focus our attention: on the role of staff and management, on the work process and job designs of operators, on the restrictive management practices, or on the reward system?" Finally, relevance leads us to ask, "What is the technology we have that could be applied to bring about positive change?"

At the same time we were searching for relevance we were paying attention to timeliness and fit. Considering timeliness required that we be practical about the time and other resources available to introduce and implement change. In the face of current work demands, was there any possibility to convene operators for training over an extended period of time? Would the necessary staff and management resources be available to create and sustain literacy? Would the financial resources be provided to support changes?

Fit required that we be realistic about opposition to change. The system currently operating in the plant did not come about accidentally. It was built on a foundation of control and consistency. Everyone from the plant manager to the last operator hired participated in and sustained it. Would the organization be open to a fundamental change? Would the notion of distributing power in service of the business have any viability?

Frequently when there is high relevance there are substantial fit issues. With this particular client we thought we had high relevance. We believed there were numerous opportunities to apply our expertise in a way that would build capacity in the plant. Creating business literacy, redesigning the jobs and work flows, redefining the role of staff and supervision, all seemed to offer the promise of improved business results.

At the same time there were serious fit issues. There was strong commitment to the existing system. There were doubts the organization would support or create the conditions necessary to implement the use of our expertise successfully.

The feedback meeting where all this would be discussed with the client would be difficult.

THE ADVERTISING GROUP CASE STUDY

An advertising group was facing serious and dramatic change. As a result of its early work, it had moved toward breaking the department into self-managed businesses. Each business focused on particular categories of advertisers such as car dealers, furniture stores, and financial services. The group saw each of these internal businesses as responsible for a particular segment of the customer market. The staff of each business set itsown goals and objectives for revenues and expenses, and was eager to be accountable for results achieved at the end of the year. Blocking success were current management practices and policies. There were tight restrictions about who could see financial information. Performance reviews were controlled by Human Resources.

The group knew that if it couldn't get timely measures about its progress in managing a particular market segment, it would have a difficult time making sound business decisions: where to use its resources, where to increase or decrease effort, where and when to focus attention. Furthermore, even if it could gain access to the information, it was currently aggregated in a way that was meaningful only to senior management. Within the larger organization there was no resource available that could focus attention on creating useful measures for small core work units on a timely basis. Historically, Finance staff members didn't see it as their job.

The cross-functional staff group consulting to the advertising groups—Human Resources, Finance, and Information Systems—asked itself whether there was an opportunity here to bring in practices and processes that would increase the capacity of these advertising businesses to manage themselves. Could staff help build systems that would distribute financial literacy to the internal businesses, giving them the useful measures they need in order to make sound business decisions? If such changes could be made, the advertising groups could take accountability for the management of their business.

Performance reviews provided another opportunity. Current practice required use of a particular form, a certain timetable, and a set of specific procedures.

As the advertising group moved toward redefining itself as a business at risk with each member choosing for accountability, the idea of a manager evaluating each of them individually ran counter to the members' intention. "What we need," they realized, "is a method for dealing with performance issues in a way that we can demonstrate our accountability to the business and to each other."

Relevance required an answer to the question "Can we help them construct a performance review practice that will embody their intention to be accountable to the business and to each other for success and failure?"

The staff group found it could be highly relevant to this client and was happily surprised at the support it got from the client for a distributive stance. High relevance and good fit are a rare combination.

IN CONCLUSION

When we examine practices and architecture during the discovery process, we are asking the following questions: Do they reinforce the old system of centralizing power and control, or do they move toward decentralization and the wider redistribution of power? Do we have a technology that could redesign them with the promise of improved business results? Is it timely? Will the organization extend enough support to the changes that there is a reasonable chance the technology can be successfully implemented?

The discovery process is the phase where we reach a conclusion about these questions. The next phase requires conversations with a client where we discuss our conclusions and come to a joint decision about proceeding or not proceeding.

FACE TO FACE WITH MANAGEMENT PRACTICES AND CORPORATE ARCHITECTURE

This section lists some major management practices. During the discovery process, make a note of which ones are in use in the client unit, and ask the following three questions about each one: Who has the responsibility for carrying out this practice? Can others influence this practice? In this practice, is managing segregated from doing the work?

Conducting performance reviews

Making hiring decisions

Convening meetings

Raising difficult issues

Changing work processes

Modifying products and services

Managing customer relationships

Managing conflict

In the traditional system, the principle that defines and controls organizational structure is control and compliance. This principle encourages people to move toward specialization, and it allows upper management easy ways to control, measure, and reward performance. Here are some overall factors to consider when looking at organizational architecture:

Structure: How are people grouped—for customer service or internal ease of control?

Job design: Can people be innovative, make choices, assume responsibility concerning their work, and so on?

Rewards: Are rewards linked to business outcomes in the marketplace?

Management and staff roles: Are managing and doing integrated into the core work process? Does staff audit and control for compliance, or transfer expertise for self-sufficiency?

The organizational architecture is very different from the organizational chart, and you will need to talk with people at all levels of the unit to get an idea of its real form. Here are some sample questions to work into your interviews or think about during your observations to elicit information on the existing organizational architecture.

- Job Design:

    Who controls your work?

    How is it controlled?

    How is your performance measured?

    How does what you do relate to your job description?

    Are you encouraged to learn new skills and expand your ability to contribute?

    Are you encouraged to teach skills you know to others?

- Management

    Is managing separated from doing the work?

    Is "management" a class of people or a set of tasks?

- Staff Role

    Who do you think staff groups see as their client?

    What do staff groups see as their mission and purpose?

- Rewards

    Is everyone rewarded based on the unit's performance in the marketplace?

    Are rewards focused on individual or unit performance?

- Structure

    Are people grouped for customer convenience or internal ease of control?

    How does the structure support control and consistency?

    How does the structure support innovation and unique response?

CHAPTER 9

DECIDING RELEVANCE, TIMELINESS, AND FIT

By the time you've gone through the discovery process—taking time to get to know the unit and looking for opportunities to apply your technology—you have a fairly good picture of the client unit. You've looked at the ways it operates and manages itself, its policies, procedures, practices, and architecture. Some tentative conclusions about relevance, timeliness, and fit have formed in your mind.

GO OR NO-GO

In the third phase, the task is to come to a conclusion with the client about proceeding or not proceeding. This phase is also carried out in conversation. The point of this conversation is to describe the tentative conclusions reached regarding relevance, timeliness, and fit. The following list summarizes the stages of the conversation in question:

The Feedback Meeting

- Make personal contact.
- Review the contract.

Remind the client about:

    Developing an independent point of view

    Raising difficult issues

    Getting access to the data

Restate what you were assessing:

    Relevance

    Timeliness

    Fit

- Outline an agenda for the meeting.

- Focus the discussion on the most important issue:

    Relevance

    Timeliness

    Fit

- Frame the issue:

    Give the business case reasons.

    Restate the case for a distributive stance.

    Reference the information.

- Frame choices for the client.

- Come to an agreement on proceeding or terminating the work.

- Contract with the client about conditions that will support fit.

- Negotiate the specific use of your expertise:

    Interventions and outcomes expected

    Promises and guarantees

    Consequences

- Restate the agreement.

THE TRADITIONAL FEEDBACK MEETING

During the feedback phase of the traditional consulting process, the consultant brings to management's attention variances within technical processes or other problem areas and recommends solutions for them. Both sides generally expect that these solutions will involve hiring the consultant and reinforcing management's position.

For example, Information Systems would offer to fix a software application being used by a unit for a task such as retrieving manufacturing cost data. If a software design results in an inferior product, staff might recommend changing the software so the information becomes more accessible. When traditional staff groups look at a unit, they tend to see problems that are connected to what they do. From a Human Resources perspective, the staff might recommend putting a new procedure or policy in place to ensure that performance reviews are done on time, or launching some effort to develop clearer and more well-defined job descriptions, or moving to a more sophisticated form of succession planning. The purpose of their recommendations is usually to make the existing system work better. The traditional staff approach does not speak to the value of the practice or system, or to how the staff might further build capacity by applying its technology.

More basic questions are seldom heard. Is fixing the current system worth the time? Is the system itself one that adds value? Is it the best way to use our expertise? Is sustaining, fixing, or maintaining the current system and practices the best use of our expertise? Will the time, money, and energy expended create increased capacity in this business? Could our expertise be applied differently in a way that would have much greater promise of increasing business capacity? No one wants to ask. The working assumption takes the current system and use of staff expertise as a given. Staff's fundamental purpose isn't to raise doubts about whether or not the system ought to be there, but to fix it so that it operates as it's intended to operate. Historically, this phase of staff work focuses only on the application of current technology or expertise for fixing the system or replacing its parts with different ones that may do the same job better.

What is being highlighted here is a question about the underlying intent of staff groups. If most of our time and energy are spent to fix or strengthen the focus on control and consistency, does it have real business value or is it just routine behavior we do for its own sake?

THE NEW FEEDBACK MEETING

If you adopt the position suggested here, the same three key areas require attention during the feedback meeting as during the initial review—relevance, timeliness, and fit.

As noted earlier, *relevance* means that our technology can improve the business capacity of the unit. During the discovery meetings, we looked for possible applications of technology. Of course, we were also willing to look at specific problems, but our stance calls for looking at any specific problem in the context of the whole. Looking at the whole demands that we look at the entire unit's business capacity and how acting on a specific problem will increase or diminish the unit's overall capacity to succeed in the business.

During the feedback meeting, we focus attention on specific areas where we found limited capacity and where there is real chance our expertise will have an impact. Those areas may or may not be limited to the reasons that first caused us to meet with the client.

Timeliness in the context of the feedback meeting means getting straight about cost and time. Money and time are real. No matter how relevant your expertise, no matter how good the fit, if the organization will not commit to the time and dollars, you cannot proceed.

Fit here means facing the difficult issues of values and beliefs. Everyone carries into this meeting a position about what makes an organization work. It is not just an intellectual position, it is an emotional commitment. No matter how relevant or timely you believe your expertise is, it is foolish to proceed without agreement on the underlying direction. Fit confronts the issue of distributing power as a fundamental strategy for building business capacity. Those committed to consolidation of power—to caretaking, prescription, and compliance—will not in the end support a distributive strategy.

Coming to terms with relevance, timeliness, and fit is the work of this meeting.

THE SEWING LINE: MAKING THE CASE FOR RELEVANCE

After the discovery process described in Chapter Eight, I met with the clothing manufacturer's management. We discussed my group's conclusions about relevance, timeliness, and fit.

Here is how I made the case for relevance: "I think it is very important to create literacy about the business throughout the entire plant. Operators need to know that their jobs are at risk. They need to be told that, given current production levels, outsourcing of this plant's product is a likely possibility. They need to be told why that's true. If it is important for everyone to choose accountability for this plant, it is important to tell them the truth about how things stand. If the goal is partnership in building a viable future, critical information can't be withheld."

The second area I focused on was the distribution of choice and competence. "I don't think the issue is monitoring the operators more or making them work faster. The solution isn't more control and consistency, it's the process. The entire work process has to be changed to achieve maximum production capacity. It's not going to get any better as long as the process is done the same old way, trying to control everything each operator does. One way to think of transforming the process is to focus on distributing choice and competence. It may mean changing many management practices you currently use and the roles of operators, staff, and supervisors."

One of the managers interrupted here. "Hold on! What the hell are you talking about? Get concrete. What would change?"

I responded, "Operators might need to learn not only new sewing operations but also new management skills—the competence to manage their own work process. They would have to learn to integrate managing and doing. Supervisors would not manage workers' movements from one work station to another. Those shifts can be most easily and effectively managed if operators do it themselves. Operators know what they have to produce each day and they can move themselves around as it makes sense to them. As a team, they can actively manage rather than wait for a supervisor to notice when garments are backing up. Since they are usually first to notice a backup, they can be first to move on it."

I suggested that it might be important for engineers to teach operators their expertise so that the operators themselves would be able to look at a new garment, break it into separate operations, and figure out the best way to move it through the construction process. The mechanics would probably need to take the same approach—teaching the operators to change their own needles, for example, so they didn't sit idle by the dozen waiting for one of six pairs of hands to show up for that simple chore. The point was to transfer the expertise and competence of the engineers and mechanics to the operators so that they would be able to lay out their own construction process and maintain their own machines.

Finally, I raised the question of tying compensation to production. I explained, "If the lines are a business at risk in the marketplace, how do we create variable compensation that reflects that reality? Operators should be able to make as much as they can—but they should also be at risk when they don't produce."

The discussion continued. I tied the proposed changes to business outcomes. I was specific about how our technology could bring about the changes we were suggesting. We discussed promises and guarantees we would stand by if we decided together to proceed. The clients demanded I be clear about how the changes proposed would affect business results such as unit cost, product quality, and cycle time.

Discussing these issues is the work of demonstrating your relevance to the client's business. In discussing relevance with a client it is important to articulate it in the form of an offer, including the promise and guarantee you choose to make.

THE NEWS SUBSIDIARY: FINDING RELEVANCE

Remember Kathy, the corporate staff team, and the major newspaper? After gathering data, she and the team met with the publisher. In discussing where they would offer to do further work, Kathy talked about promises and guarantees. "If you use the methods we are proposing," she said, "here's the concrete business outcome we believe you can achieve." She then entered into a specific discussion of the business outcomes and time lines they could expect. She made several specific promises.

THE PROMISES

The first promise was that using staff expertise to create widespread literacy would result in achieving the necessary multi-million-dollar cost cuts within the required time.

The second promise was that at the end of that time each of the units would have absorbed the necessary headcount reduction and would have restructured and redesigned itself into a viable organization with the full capacity to function. The staff team wouldn't leave behind a shattered organization, unable to operate in the face of the cost cuts it had just endured. The units would come out of this process with a viable, optimistic organization ready to take on very difficult goals, missions, and responsibilities for the next business year.

The third promise was that these units, and the organization as a whole, would develop an integrated strategy for turning around declining circulation and advertising revenue at the end of this difficult period.

The staff promised that using its technology to focus on literacy and accountability would result in all these outcomes.

THE GUARANTEE

Staff members backed their promises with a guarantee. If they didn't produce, they would face consequences that they had freely chosen. There would be economic consequences: The newspaper could cancel any or all of the contracts with them at any time. Consequences also focused on their potential loss of credibility within the larger corporation. They would be evaluated in terms of how well they did or didn't do with this newspaper, and they expected that evaluation to be broadcast to all the papers in the chain. They chose for the outcomes to be public. The staff knew up front, before they did their first day of work, that their credibility and reputation were tied to a specific result.

Focusing on relevance is demanding. First, the staff must be very clear about what it can influence and what it can promise. This is the moment when staff must be prepared to turn curiosity, interest, and discussion into a concrete promise for which it chooses accountability. Second, when staff expertise is not relevant, the staff group must be prepared to admit it and bear the disappointment of not proceeding. Third, and more often than not, staff must propose applications of its expertise that will frequently surprise and often confuse the client.

TIMELINESS

The second area to discuss, before a promise is finalized, is timeliness. Timeliness leads us to ask whether the client is willing to risk sufficient dollars as well as people's time in this effort. The resolution of the issue required straight talk about the dollars and time required to move the process forward.

With the newspaper, the staff had a client facing a multimillion dollar shortfall. Everyone was pressed to the limit. Staff was proposing work that would be time-consuming and expensive. They would be an additional cost in the midst of a cost-cutting process.

CONFRONTING FIT

Fit is the most difficult issue. It may be the least discussed but most important issue to engage with a client. Most interventions by staff groups fail, not because they didn't have a relevant and timely technology, but because of poor fit. Fit is not resistance. Resistance is an indirect expression of an underlying emotional concern. Fit refers to an explicit and public position about how an organization should be managed. Fit issues are value based.

THE NEWS SUBSIDIARY: MAKING A FIT

The last item Kathy and the publisher had to discuss during the feedback meeting was the issue of fit. Kathy and the staff team came into that meeting taking a position on how their technology should be used, namely, to distribute accountability, business literacy, competence, choice, and resources. They held that distribution is the most promising means to build business capacity and the best use of their expertise.

From that stance they saw many opportunities to increase capacity. It was also clear to them that if their clients couldn't choose to embrace a wider distribution of power, despite their reservations, the hope of their technology's having impact was not only diminished, it was bound to fail.

Kathy and the staff team already had struggled with the publisher over releasing specific information about the extent of the problem. Kathy raised the issue this way: "We're proposing a distribution of power. We're talking about reversing a commitment and belief that has been central to this organization for years. This is an issue not only for the organization but for each of you personally. We are asking you to support a new stance that in many ways is contrary to what you have lived out for a long time. We can't make a promise to you about having an impact unless you are willing to embrace this approach and fully support it. We are looking for a basic and sincere willingness to give this approach an opportunity to work."

Here are some of the exchanges they had:

The publisher replied, "The fit issue. If I understand you correctly, I personally need to adopt your viewpoint. Sounds pretty theoretical to me. What in the world is it you want me to do?"

"We have watched you struggle with whether or not you were going to tell people the million-dollar number," Kathy replied. "If you want to know concretely what we mean by taking the distributive stance, it means continuing to tell people the difficult truths. It can't be a one-time event. Of course, simply telling people will not make them literate about the business, but it is a clear indication of your willingness to move toward the distribution of business literacy within the organization. Are you willing to continue to put the harsh reality out there? Are you willing to let everyone in this organization always know the extent of the problem? Are you willing to let *them* engage it on both a personal level and on a business level?"

She went on, "If you use our technology, literacy is only a first step. We are going to put *choice* into the hands of the various divisions and departments. It is going to be their responsibility to find the millions of dollars that they've got to find within their own departments in order to cut costs. We want to put into their hands the *power* to make those choices. They will start from the bottom up and redesign their entire department. The choice about how they are going to manage it will be primarily in their hands. That's contrary to how you have dealt with such issues in the past. Historically, you would take the senior management group off site for two or three days to make these decisions for them. With the approach we are suggesting, it becomes the departments' responsibility to redesign their organizations. For you to let go of making these decisions for them will be a big leap. Are you willing to distribute these choices to the organization to be acted on by hundreds of people over a period of months? Can you work up enough trust and enough will to make that move?

"If you are not willing to support this direction, stop now, because we don't believe we will have a positive impact unless you can."

The publisher of this paper is one of the warmest, brightest, and most gregarious people I have met. He is also one of the most committed "caretakers" of people. Everyone he meets with leaves his office feeling comforted, secure, understood, and in some way loved. Kathy's last statement to him was personal. "Pete, perhaps there is no more concrete way to communicate what you will have to do than to talk about how you are with people. What's important in this approach is for you to do much less caretaking and protecting. Your conversations need to focus on the harsh realities and people's individual responsibility for dealing with them. People are going to leave your office disappointed and unsettled. That will be a lot for you to deal with.

"It's our job to provide the technology to make it happen. But you have to *agree* to make it happen, advocate for it, and choose to be accountable for taking this position."

Those were the fit issues Kathy raised. Even though she saw relevance for staff expertise, if the publisher, the president, and the key players in this organization would not support this specific approach, it wouldn't matter what they did. They would fail because the conditions necessary to support the use of staff technology would not exist.

A Postscript: "Don't tap-dance on my head about your happiness."

A few days later Kathy attended a large group meeting of the organization. Its purpose was to discuss all the difficult issues that were at hand. The fit issue was still unresolved. During the meeting Pete met with every major department. He heard person after person talk of their pain, anxiety, and disappointment in the face of these issues. He tried to make it all right, offering reassurance and promises of a brighter future. He didn't want anyone to leave feeling unhappy or discouraged. He saw him-self as responsible for fixing it all and creating hope.

After two days of these conversations, something changed for him. He asked to speak just as the meeting was about to end. Everyone expected an inspirational talk. It didn't come in the form anyone anticipated. Pete began, "I have heard from many of you during the last two days. Everyone is hurting. Everyone wishes all this would go away, including me! Everyone, includ-ing me, wants me to fix it. I can't. Please don't tap-dance on my head about your happiness. I can't make anybody happy or excited about what we are facing. I have a hard enough time dealing with it myself. Each of us has to decide how we want to deal with all of this. The choice is helplessness and despair, or hope and optimism. It's in your hands. It's in my hands. Each of us stands alone making that choice. No one can do it for us." When he finished the entire group rose and applauded him for five full minutes. For Kathy it was a demonstration that fit was possible—not guaranteed, but possible.

THE SECURITY AND SAFETY ISSUE

Staff groups and consultants find it difficult to raise fit issues with the client. It may mean putting the contract on the line. If the client says, "Well OK, I'm for some literacy, but I don't want to tell anybody specific numbers," the way Kathy's publisher did, it's enormously tempting to say, "You don't have to tell anyone the exact number if you don't want to. You don't have to tell them it means this much in headcount. And you don't have to tell them that if this trend continues, they are going to face the same thing again next year." Instead, it is tempting to do some basic training around profit and loss statements and call it literacy.

These kinds of activities might look like distributing literacy. Nonetheless, they have nothing to do with telling the real business story about this organization at this moment.

PRESENTING RELEVANCE, TIMELINESS, AND FIT TO CORE WORKERS

Conversations around relevance, timeliness, and fit are held not only with those who manage but also with those who are being managed. It means presenting everyone with the same picture: "Here are places in the organization where we think we can make a difference in dealing with what you are facing."

The set of questions raised with people in the core work process may be different, but they are still fit issues: Are you willing to give up your cynicism? Are you willing to let go of the conversations that begin with "This is a horrible place to work" and "It's unjust and it's unfair" and "This business is no longer what it used to be" and "If only we had better managers" and "If only our owners were not so money hungry, things would be better"?

Are you willing to choose for optimism and accountability for the business? Are you willing to make your choices real in terms of what you choose to learn, what you choose to manage, what you choose to take accountability for? Because if you are willing to become business literate, willing to learn new things, and willing to manage as well as do your work, we think that the changes proposed will make real and positive change. If not, you can go through endless training sessions and nothing will happen.

Another Example of the "Fit" Discussion

For several weeks, I had been talking with Steve, a senior manager of a major bank, about the activities we thought would build capacity. When I first entered into the fit discussions, he said, "Well, I really don't understand your 'new stance,' but I like what you are proposing to do. Proceed with it." At that time, I didn't have any information that told me there was a serious fit issue with him.

I soon noticed, however, that Steve's name kept coming up as someone with very mixed feelings about moving in the distributive direction. I heard him voicing increased reservations. Something was not going well. I decided to meet with him.

What Steve liked about the technology being introduced was its focus on accountability. What I didn't catch earlier was the meaning he gave to the word. He explained, "This is an effort that focuses on *holding* people accountable. That means taking names and kicking butt, and I'm just the man who can do that. It fits with my values and my understanding of accountability. For a long time I have wanted to have some very direct conversations with people and felt prevented from doing so. Around here it is more important to be polite than honest. But now with a focus on accountability, I can tell them the truth."

He went on to talk about his recent experience. "Here are the things I'm doing. I'm requiring my direct reports to meet with me every week for an hour to update me on everything they are doing. Before they decide on anything serious, I'm requiring they come to me to sign off. I'm staying on top of them like glue, and what I'm getting back from them is a lot of resistance. They are accusing me of not understanding what I'm supposed to be doing and of getting in the way of this process."

What Steve didn't get about accountability is that this effort isn't about holding people accountable at all. It's about each individual *choosing* for accountability—which is a different matter entirely.

At the end of our conversation, I said to him, "Steve, what we have here is a fit issue. *Holding* people accountable and building systems to hold people accountable is what you have been doing for years. You're good at it. You're simply trying harder to be better. In contrast, I'm talking about creating a system where people themselves *choose* for accountability. You know how to build an organization where people are *held* accountable. The question for you is, Are you willing to move toward creating an organization where people in the ranks *choose* for accountability with as much enthusiasm, energy, and sense of responsibility as you have? This is a wholly different way of working with people. The value in a distributive system is not in how many people you can hold accountable, your value is in how successful you can be in creating an organization where everyone chooses accountability."

With Steve there was no conversion experience. He struggled with this issue every day. Fit doesn't demand conversion; it just requires people to choose to go in this direction recognizing that very little of life happens in a straight line.

TAKING THE RISK OF GIVING HONEST FEEDBACK

Feedback discussions of relevance, timeliness, and fit can threaten your future employment. At the conclusion of these discussions, if you can't see any relevance, there is no promise you can make. If your interventions would not be timely, there is no promise you can make. Finally, if the client is unwilling to create the conditions that support fit through acts of will that allow your technology to be used successfully, there is no promise you can make.

Once you risk taking a position about how your technology should be used to build capacity, you confront very personal issues about values, about long-held beliefs and attitudes. At times it feels like selling revolution to the ruling class.

For a staff group or consultant, the alternative is to avoid taking a position on fit and to see yourself as only a provider of a technical service to a manager and business unit for which you are not accountable. Such a stance leads to a very different kind of discussion.

The discussion with Steve would never have occurred in my former consulting practice. All I would have wanted from Steve was support for doing our program within the organization. As long as there was a yes to that, I would have felt successful. I would never have taken accountability. I would never have asked myself, "Do I believe the way my technology is being used by this organization is going to have a positive business impact? Do I believe that Steve and other members of this organization will create the conditions that support the use of the technology?"

IN CONCLUSION

There are lessons to be learned from these stories.

First, if I am a business at risk in the marketplace, I had better make only those promises I have a high probability of keeping.

Second, I am not free to ignore the conditions under which I am trying to implement my technology because those conditions will determine whether or not I am successful.

Third, it's an act of courage to deal with these issues.

There is nothing cosmetic about these conversations. All the discussions around being a business at risk, making an offer, issuing a guarantee, saying no, and mastering a technology are at the center of the feedback meeting. I have to articulate where I see opportunity and exactly how I would go about building capacity. I've got to be able to make connections for clients in their language that lets them see how the improvements might occur—how using this technology leads to increased ability to offer a unique response to the customer, cut costs, reduce cycle time, and improve quality. I've got to raise difficult issues about fit with the clients. I've got to confront those issues with good will.

To talk about being at risk as a theory is one thing. To live it out face to face in direct conversations is quite another thing. It means talking about issues that are usually not confronted. Such conversations are fundamental to discovering whether or not I can offer anything of value.

Everything up to this moment of the feedback meeting has been preparation for me to say what needs to be said in the room with the client sitting in front of me. It is all on the line.

CONFRONTING FIT IN THE FEEDBACK MEETING

What follows is an outline and explanation of a feedback meeting where fit is the central issue to be confronted. It differs in some important aspects from the general feedback meeting outline at the beginning of the chapter. I use it for an example because I believe the fit issue is the most difficult one to confront.

The Fit Feedback Meeting

- Review the contract.

  Remind the client about:

  > Developing an independent point of view
  > Raising difficult issues
  > Getting access to the data

  Restate what you were assessing:

  > Relevance
  > Timeliness
  > Fit

- Outline an agenda for the meeting.
- Make a good faith statement about relevance and timeliness.
- Focus the discussion on the fit issue.
- Frame the fit issue.

  > Give the business case reasons.
  > Restate the case for a distributive stance.
  > Reference the information.
  > Frame choices for the client about fit.

- Come to an agreement on proceeding or terminating the work.
- Contract with the client about creating fit.
- Negotiate the specific use of your expertise.

  > Interventions and outcomes expected

> Promises and guarantees
>
> Consequences
>
> • Restate the agreement.

STEP 1: MAKE PERSONAL CONTACT

Choose for good will.

Good will is coming to the meeting choosing to help the client and unit succeed, and assuming your client is acting with good intentions.

STEP 2: REVIEW THE CONTRACT

Remind the clients of the agreements about independent points of view, raising difficult issues, and so on.

STEP 3: OUTLINE AN AGENDA FOR THE MEETING

It reduces anxiety when the client understands the plan for the meeting.

STEP 4: MAKE A GOOD FAITH STATEMENT ABOUT RELEVANCE AND TIMELINESS

Good faith means you give a clear and simple picture of where your expertise could have an impact. "Here are two or three areas—accountability and business literacy—where we can make an impact on the business issues you are most concerned about."

STEP 5: FOCUS THE DISCUSSION ON FIT

Start by framing the fit issue. What is the business case for wider distribution of accountability, literacy, choice, capacity, resources, and competence, as it relates to my expertise within this unit?

What is the information I want to refer to here?

For example: "Here's the way I see the fit issue. We have methods and a technology that could be very relevant here for increasing capacity. How our technology is used is a critical issue for us. Our bias is to move the organization toward the distribution of accountability, business literacy, choice, competence, and resources. If it is your belief that control is the best strategy to increase capacity, then we have a fit issue. The data tell us there is a strong preference for control, consistency, and compliance as a management strategy in this unit."

Reference the data—that is, describe the factual situation that supports your conclusion. For example: "Distribution of literacy and choice while focusing on accountability will improve the ability of your unit to respond to customers."

Frame choices for the client about fit. Make sure their choice is not just a cosmetic act, a nonchoice with no commitment behind it. You can test its genuineness in the next few steps.

If you get a yes, don't presume the client has had a religious conversion about distribution. Don't expect they will do everything you recommend all at once. Most will be willing to take just the first step.

Confront the client with the choice. Let the choice be free. Do not get in the way.

Consultants are frequently tempted to do one or several of the following when confronting the fit issue:

- Selling the idea
- Bartering or trading this for that
- Arguing or debating
- Making a deal
- Promising

Framing the choice for the client involves explaining to the client what the choice for distribution entails. This is very different from arguing, bartering, promising, or making a deal to get the client to choose for distribution.

STEP 6: COME TO AN AGREEMENT ON PROCEEDING OR TERMINATING THE WORK

When presented with this choice, the client is bound to get anxious. Almost any important change is preceded by tension. As a consultant, you welcome the tension. It is a sign that the client really sees what the choice is and what it implies.

Here is a moment in the meeting when you will be tempted to manage the relationship and reduce tension. Stay with the tension. Stay focused on the fact that the client must make a choice.

This is a moment of risk for you, too. If the client says no, then the meeting is essentially over. As a consultant committed to building capacity in the organization, you cannot make any promise that your expertise, even if used, will make a difference. Without closing the fit gap it would be a waste of the client's time and money.

If you and the client don't agree on fit issues, proceeding would be a waste of time. In fact, proceeding in such a case would amount to you taking responsibility for your client's success without conditions to support that success. Can you deliver?

STEP 7: CONTRACT WITH THE CLIENT ABOUT CREATING FIT

You and the client must come to an agreement about the conditions that need to be put in place by the client and the unit to support your technology.

STEP 8: NEGOTIATE THE SPECIFIC USE OF YOUR EXPERTISE

Propose an intervention. Come to an agreement on where and how you will apply your expertise and the outcomes expected.

Make promises. With the client you must commit to an agreed-upon set of business results.

Offer a guarantee. You will want to offer a guarantee, in case your results do not meet your promises. Find a guarantee that is agreeable to your client and shows that you have entered these negotiations choosing accountability for your business impact.

Clarify consequences. Choose consequences if you do not keep your promise. For example, you might offer to forfeit your consulting fee or a portion of it. You may elect to find other consultants who can do what needs to be done.

This is not about falling on your sword. It is a way of showing the client that you too have something at risk. It is the opposite of "I'm here to help. You are at risk."

It is not enough to guarantee that you will "give a good workshop" or "try hard."

STEP 9: RESTATE THE AGREEMENT

Go over the various points and actions that you and your client have agreed to. Make sure that each side understands and accepts what the other plans to do.

CHAPTER 10

THE PATH OF COMMITMENT

This book has argued for the transformation of staff groups, particularly staff groups within large organizations. It has focused on two key changes. The first is that staff groups choose accountability in three areas:

- For the impact they have on their clients' critical business issues

- For mastering an expertise that will contribute to building the capacity of client units to survive and prosper in the marketplace

- For taking a position and making explicit the conditions a client must create and support for staff expertise to have positive impact

The choice for accountability in these three areas is central and essential to the change.

The other major choice required for the change advocated here is to embrace a deeper and broader mission—the distribution throughout the client organization of the components of organizational power:

business literacy, accountability, choice, competence, and access to resources.

Making these choices is an act of service to the organization. The orientation they reflect is fundamental to building business capacity within client organizations.

GOOD STAFF WORK

It has been the book's purpose to offer an alternative view of what *good* staff work means. Good staff work is not, at its heart, just managing the relationship with the client, although that has its place. It is not just doing what clients want in the name of "delighting" them, building trust, relieving tension or creating comfort. Good staff work is not being satisfied with carrying out programs, processes, activities, and mandates. It is not keeping expertise complex, hidden, and inaccessible.

Good staff work:

- Chooses accountability for creating a service business that has demonstrable value and impact on a client's business results.

- Knows and delivers something of value to the success of the organization.

- Is honest with the client about what can be accomplished and under what conditions.

- Puts the staff unit at risk by choosing to make promises about results and choosing consequences for not delivering. Good staff work involves issuing real guarantees!

- Says no to work when the staff expertise is not relevant, when it's the wrong time to apply it, or when the client insists on using it in a way that will ensure its failure.

- Gives up dearly loved programs, services, and products when they no longer meet a real business need.

- Seeks risk more than safety as a service to clients. It takes the chances, names the difficult issues, and acknowledges its own limitations and failures.

- Seeks no place at the business table unless there is something to contribute. Good staff work seeks not so much the sanction of senior management as the opportunity to demonstrate worth to its clients.

- Is committed to contributing more than to watching.
- Is dedicated to keeping service expertise understandable, accessible, and transferable.

JUDY: ACCOUNTABILITY AND CHANGE

What Judy taught me was the difference between *being held accountable* and *choosing accountability*. It is the difference between living a life based on what I am obliged to do and on what I willingly and freely choose to do.

In a world where we are holding others accountable or are being held accountable, none of us owns our own lives. Accountability becomes a demand for compliance, something I have to do because it is demanded. In a world where accountability is imposed I am never accountable, for I have never chosen it as my own. I may comply, but I am not accountable. In such a world I never lay claim to my own life. In some very basic way, I remain always a child. With this choice goes all the childish behaviors and childish fears: blaming, helplessness, excuses, and the endless search for the easy path. To live in this world is to seek comfort, not passion.

To choose accountability freely, to choose it without barter and regardless of the outcomes, is to grow up. It is to own and lay claim to my life. Whatever the consequence of my choices, success or failure, they are mine. The life I live is not someone else's; it is mine. It is only in this world that passion is possible.

To remain married to Judy required that I grow up and take accountability for my own commitment and optimism. It required that I deal with my own disappointments. It required that I do all this without barter.

These difficult truths and choices that invaded my personal life also invaded my work life. I could approach work as something "I had to do." I could choose to view my work life as a world where I was *held* accountable and

> *As a consultant or staff person, you pay a heavy price in a business relationship if you barter, trade, sell, argue, or promise.*

all that goes with that stance: the complying, the blaming, the helpless-ness, the seeking safety. Or I could choose for accountability in my work—take the stance and take the risk.

Service people and groups have this same choice. I am absolutely convinced that the marketplace will choose those who embrace account-ability and demand it of themselves. It is these individuals and groups who will find passion and success.

I am further convinced that the marketplace will choose to do busi-ness with organizations that choose accountability for the services and products they offer. Businesses can only offer that which they can live out. In the end, all this is not just a question for the staff person or staff group. *It is a question for every business and every person in the workplace.*

The changes proposed here are radical. They demand taking a stance on unfamiliar ground. They require a commitment to an uncertain future. They make absolutely clear that safety and security are only real-ized through one's own ability to create value for others; they are not the result of seeking sanction and caretaking from others. There is no promise or guarantee provided in making the choice.

IN CONCLUSION

My belief is that the marketplace is demanding this step and that the human spirit, at its best, longs for it. As Judy made clear to me, "You have a choice."

Sources and Inspirations

Many authors have deeply influenced my thinking over the last twenty years. This list is not exhaustive; there are others who might well have been mentioned. However, it does identify those who were critical to the development of the ideas contained in this book, which sort into two areas—personal change and the role of service groups in complex organizations.

Personal Change

For me philosophy has offered more enlightenment about the struggle to change than any other academic discipline.

No single book has influenced me more than Martin Heidegger's *Being and Time*. He was, in my opinion, the first of the modern philosophers to rediscover the individual and the first-person perspective that is so critical to managing change.

Heidegger's teacher was Edmund Husserl, the father of the epistemological method called *phenomenology*. *The Paris Lectures* by Husserl, translated by Peter Koestenbaum, describes this method in as direct and simple a way as is possible. Understanding phenomenology is a key to understanding Heidegger's thinking and change from a first-person perspective.

Heidegger is very tough reading. Commentaries were essential for me to grasp an understanding of his work. Although the book is somewhat dated, I found Michael Gelvin's *A Commentary on Heidegger's "Being and Time"* to be especially helpful.

Equally powerful in understanding the individual and change is Victor Frankl's *Man's Search for Meaning*. I know of no more powerful or eloquent statement of the choices faced by the individual in the midst of radical change.

David Whyte's poetry has been significant in my grasping the experience of the individual through a different voice—the voice of the poet.

Songs for Coming Home and *Where Many Rivers Meet* are two of his collections I would recommend to anyone.

THE ROLE OF STAFF IN COMPLEX ORGANIZATIONS

Peter Block has long been a friend and collaborator. His three books are all relevant to the subject matter of this book. *Flawless Consulting* is a classic in defining the staff consulting role. *The Empowered Manager* and *Stewardship* contributed directly to the thinking about stance that is central to redefining the staff role.

Core competence is a revolutionary concept authored by Gary Hamel and C. K. Prahalad. Their book *Competing for the Future* is the best source for understanding this idea in depth.

A Nation of Victims by Charles Sykes is a wonderful commentary on human nature and contemporary American character. His ideas illuminate the love affair with "caretaking" and upward-serving behavior that is so deeply embedded in the modern organization.

John Micklethwait and Adrian Wooldridge have recently published a book titled *The Witch Doctors*. It is a wonderful review of the current thinking being offered to organizations by management gurus. I particularly like it because it points out in a gentle and humorous way the flaws and shortcomings contained in much of the wisdom gurus' sales pitches. It is useful in understanding the advice-giving role in which staff groups find themselves.

OTHER FORCES

Others have deeply influenced my thinking by deed and word. They have not put pen to paper to record their wisdom. They should. Again, the list is not exhaustive. It is a first step in my acknowledging all those who have contributed unselfishly to this book and to whatever insights I have gained about service and change.

Joan Arnold lives and works in Roswell, New Mexico. Her tough and uncommon faith in what is possible for each and every person regardless of position, status, or rank helped to cure my elitism. She restored my confidence and belief in myself and others.

Bob Hall is the publisher of the *Philadelphia Inquirer* and *Philadelphia Daily News*. There are unexpected moments in life when a sentence is spoken and everything changes. I was privileged to witness one of those moments with Bob. He taught me what "grace under fire" looks like. He is a living example of what it requires to persist in the face of disappointment and seemingly impossible circumstances.

Judy Henning is my wife and best friend. She has always understood that it is not what you demand for yourself that counts but what you offer others. She has been eternally patient and forgiving with me. She has never lost her optimism and commitment.

Kay Henry has lived and worked all her life in New York City. She was my first client. She took me and Human Resources seriously when both lacked credibility. Clients really have taught me everything I know—and no one taught me more than Kay.

Marge McCollum is a staff member at Knight Ridder. She is without pretense in a world where so many others seek pomp and position. Firm in her intentions, gentle in manner, and generous in spirit she is a testimony to what is possible when one chooses service over cynicism and self-absorption.

Lee Smith is the former president of Levi Strauss International. He is one of a handful of executives I knew who took a corporate values statement seriously. He understood that packaging really is not the point. He is an eloquent and graceful human being who has forsaken status and privilege to live out what he believes about contribution and service. I am privileged to call him mentor and friend.

Newman Walker is a lifelong friend and colleague. As superintendent, he shepherded the Louisville, Kentucky, school system through the changes brought about by implementing a massive desegregation plan. We all weathered that storm because of his unyielding belief in the capacity of human beings to choose for service and "the good." He resisted all efforts to surrender to paranoia and fear.

John and Joyce Weir have spent their lives in service of others. They offer workshops on their own and through the National Training Labs (NTL). Their work and lives are based on faith in the human spirit and its unlimited capacity for learning, generosity, and service. No one has a clearer or more defined understanding of accountability and its place in our lives. No one else brings more wit, curiosity, intelligence, and vitality to the living of life.

ABOUT THE AUTHOR

JOEL HENNING has worked with and for complex organizations for the last thirty years. His early experience included line management responsibilities at Montgomery Ward and Household Finance.

His introduction to the chaos and difficulty of change occurred during the early 1970s when he joined the Louisville, Kentucky, school district. In the first phase of this work he developed strategies and training programs to help turn around all the problems associated with predominately black inner city school districts at that time: racial isolation, poor academic performance, high student drop-out rates and rapidly declining staff morale. The second phase of his work involved the design and implementation of a desegregation plan that resulted in the integration and merger of the Louisville system with the nearly all-white Jefferson County school district—resulting in a single district of some 120,000 students. Finding ways to deal with the inevitable conflict, confusion, and fear between and among all groups—students, staff, and parents— became his work during this very difficult transformation. He later became the assistant superintendent of human resources and then assistant superintendent of schools in Palo Alto, California, at a time when state courts required California school districts to equalize student expenditures—more difficult and complex change.

In 1980, Joel formed his own consulting and training firm. Shortly thereafter, his firm affiliated with Designed Learning, an association that continues to this day. During that time he worked with staff groups in a wide variety of organizations, including Knight Ridder, Stanford University, Sandia Labs, Ford Motors, Bank of America, Metropolitan Life, Levi Strauss, and Equitable. This work is the raw material upon which this book, *The Future of Staff Groups: Daring to Distribute Power and Capacity*, is based.

Joel earned a doctorate in the areas of learning theory and the philosophy of education after joint studies at the University of Kentucky and the University of Florida.

Joel may be reached at:

Designed Learning, Inc.
313 South Avenue
Suite 202
Fanwood, NJ 07023
Phone: (908) 889-0300
Fax: (908) 889-4995

About Designed Learning

Designed Learning, Inc. (DL), provides customized training and consulting to organizations wanting to create high-service workplaces. It is committed to building the capacity of organizations to succeed through the broad distribution of power—business literacy, choice, access to resources, competence and accountability.

DL has developed a unique expertise in working with staff groups determined to provide the best possible service to their customers. It believes the staff role will become increasingly important in the years ahead as business looks to take advantage of new knowledge and technologies.

Staff Consulting Skills (SCS) was Designed Learning's first product. Through the years its relevance and reputation grew. Its applications were customized for a wide range of service groups including Human Resources, Information Systems, Finance, Quality, and others. SCS has become the standard by which all like courses are measured. It continues to emphasize this core competence in consulting and in Advanced Consulting Skills, a new workshop based upon this book.

Should you wish to attend public sessions or discuss how Designed Learning's workshops and consulting fit your organization's needs, please call or write:

Designed Learning, Inc.
313 South Avenue
Suite 202
Fanwood, NJ 07023
Phone: (908) 889-0300
Fax: (908) 889-4995

Index

Accommodation, 28
Accountability, xii, 63–64, 66, 167
  of business units, 29, 81, 107
  choosing, 9, 153, 163
  as component of offers, 49–51
  as component of power, 17, 68, 70
  news subsidiary case study, 120–22
  personal, 1–10, 17, 61–62
Advertising group case study, 136–37
Application and theories, 96, 97
Arnold, Joan, 166
Asset distribution, 29
Attitude surveys, 19, 47, 105, 128
Audit group case study, 34–35
Auditing, 24, 25, 32, 36

Bank of America, 169
Bankers, 28–30
  in CAD/CAM group, 31–33
  conversations with, 30
  responsibilities of, 29
Barter, 8, 94, 163
"Bean counters," xi, 63
Being and Time (Heidegger), 165
Benefits, 53
Bias, hidden, 117, 130
Block, Peter
  Flawless Consulting, 166
  Stewardship, 166
  The Empowered Manager, 166
Budget–building process, 20, 55, 128
Building capacity. *See* Capacity building
Building teams. *See* Team building
Bus driver story, 70, 106, 107
Business at risk, 28, 34, 37
Business literacy, 49, 119–20
  and capacity building, 120
  as component of power, 17, 68, 70
  distribution of, 75–78, 107

and Finance groups, 56, 57, 59, 72, 84
and Information Systems, 68–69, 72, 80–81
in sewing line example, 133–34, 144–46
in social contract, 125
Business resources. *See* Resources
Business results, 65, 66, 138
  and Finance groups, 21, 59
  and Human Resources, 20, 47
  and Information Systems, 21
  in sewing line example, 146
  and staff groups, 1, 16, 19, 26
Business units, 29. *See also* Core work units
Bystanders, 122

CAD/CAM group
  bankers and customers, 31–33
  building an offer, 53–55
  case study, 22–23
  changing conversations, 38–40
  choosing consequences, 65
  See also Engineering
Capacity building
  and business literacy, 120
  and components of power, 69
  and core competencies, 83, 86
  definition of, 16, 17, 119
  by staff groups, 27–28, 30
Capital appreciation, 28
Career tracks, 8
Caretaking, 34, 150, 166
  and bankers, 30
  elimination of, 103, 164
  and Human Resources, 37
  techniques of, 98
Centralization of power, 17, 68. *See also* Power
Change management consulting, 174
Change in staff groups, xii, 25, 27, 161. *See also* Personal change
Choice

Berrett-Koehler Publishers

BERRETT-KOEHLER is an independent publisher of books, periodicals, and other publications at the leading edge of new thinking and innovative practice on work, business, management, leadership, stewardship, career development, human resources, entrepreneurship, and global sustainability.

Since the company's founding in 1992, we have been committed to supporting the movement toward a more enlightened world of work by publishing books, periodicals, and other publications that help us to integrate our values with our work and work lives, and to create more humane and effective organizations.

We have chosen to focus on the areas of work, business, and organizations, because these are central elements in many people's lives today. Furthermore, the work world is going through tumultuous changes, from the decline of job security to the rise of new structures for organizing people and work. We believe that change is needed at all levels—individual, organizational, community, and global—and our publications address each of these levels.

We seek to create new lenses for understanding organizations, to legitimize topics that people care deeply about but that current business orthodoxy censors or considers secondary to bottom-line concerns, and to uncover new meaning, means, and ends for our work and work lives.

See next page for other books from Berrett-Koehler Publishers

Other leading-edge business books
from Berrett-Koehler Publishers

Stewardship
Choosing Service Over Self-Interest
Peter Block

BLOCK SHOWS HOW to recreate our workplaces by replacing self-interest, dependency, and control with service, responsibility, and partnership. He demonstrates how a far-reaching redistribution of power, privilege, and wealth will radically change all areas of organizational governance, and shows why this is our best hope to enable democracy to thrive.

Paperback, 288 pages, 3/96 • ISBN 1-881052-86-9
Item no. 52869-212 $16.95
Hardcover, 7/93 • ISBN 1-881052-28-1 • **Item no. 52281-212 $27.95**

The Intelligent Organization
Engaging the Talent and Initiative of Everyone in the Workplace
Gifford and Elizabeth Pinchot

THIS BOOK shows how to replace bureaucracy with more humane and effective systems for organizing and coordinating work. Gifford and Elizabeth Pinchot show how, by developing and engaging the intelligence, business judgment, and wide-system responsibility of all its members, an organization can respond more effectively to customers, partners, and competitors.

Paperback, 420 pages, 10/96 • ISBN 1-881052-98-2
Item no. 52982-212 $19.95
Hardcover, 3/94 • ISBN 1-881052-34-6 • **Item no. 52346-212 $24.95**

The New Management
Democracy and Enterprise Are Transforming Organizations

William E. Halal

TODAY'S MANAGERS are confronted with a bewildering blur of change, ranging from downsizing to spirituality. *The New Management* cuts through the confusion by integrating emerging practices into a coherent, clarifying whole. Drawing on hundreds of examples from progressive companies, an international survey of 426 managers, and economic trends, Halal shows how institutions are being transformed for the Information Age.

Hardcover, 300 pages, 5/96 • ISBN 1-881052-53-2
Item no. 52532-212 $29.95

Available at your favorite bookstore, or call (800) 929-2929

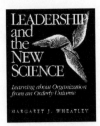

Leadership and the New Science
Learning about Organization
from an Orderly Universe

Margaret J. Wheatley

"The Best Management Book of the Year!"

—*Industry Week* magazine survey by Tom Brown

OUR UNDERSTANDING of the universe is being radically altered by the "New Science"—the revolutionary discoveries in quantum physics, chaos theory, and evolutionary biology that are overturning the prevailing models of science. Now, in this pioneering book, Wheatley shows how the new science provides equally powerful insights for changing how we design, lead, manage, and view organizations.

Paperback, 172 pages, 3/94 • ISBN 1-881052-44-3
Item no. 52443-212 $15.95
Hardcover, 9/92 • ISBN 1-881052-01-X • **Item no. 5201X-212 $24.95**

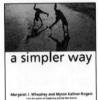

A Simpler Way

Margaret J. Wheatley and Myron Kellner-Rogers

A SIMPLER WAY is the widely awaited new book from Margaret J. Wheatley, author of the bestselling *Leadership and the New Science.* Here, Wheatley and Kellner-Rogers draw on the work of scientists, philosophers, poets, novelists, spiritual teachers, colleagues, audiences, and each other in search of new ways of understanding life and how organizing activities occur. *A Simpler Way* presents a profoundly different world view that changes how we live our lives and how we can create organizations that thrive.

Hardcover, 168 pages, 9/96 • ISBN 1-881052-95-8
Item no. 52958-212 $27.95

Seeing Systems
Unlocking the Mysteries of Organizational Life

Barry Oshry

OSHRY EXPLAINS why so many of our efforts to create more satisfying and productive human systems end in disappointment, lost opportunities, broken relationships, and failed partnerships. He provides us with a new set of lenses with which to view these systemic relationships and patterns, enabling us to recognize and stop destructive patterns of behavior.

Paperback, 225 pages, 9/96 • ISBN 1-881052-99-0
Item no. 52990-212 $22.95

Available at your favorite bookstore, or call (800) 929-2929

The Fourth Wave
Business in the 21st Century

Herman Bryant Maynard, Jr. and Susan E. Mehrtens

APPLYING THE CONCEPT of historical waves originally propounded by Alvin Toffler in *The Third Wave,* Herman Maynard and Susan Mehrtens look toward the next century and foresee a "fourth wave," an era of integration and responsibility far beyond Toffler's revolutionary description of third-wave postindustrial society. They examine how business has changed in the second and third waves and must continue to change in the fourth. The changes concern the basics—how an institution is organized, how it defines wealth, how it relates to surrounding communities, how it responds to environmental needs, and how it takes part in the political process.

Paperback, 236 pages, 7/96 • ISBN 1-57675-002-7
Item no. 50027-212 $18.95
Hardcover, 6/93 • ISBN 1-881052-15-X • **Item no. 5215X-212 $28.95**

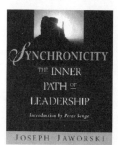

Synchronicity
The Inner Path of Leadership

Joseph Jaworski

SYNCHRONICITY is an inspirational guide to developing the most essential leadership capacity for our time: the ability to collectively shape our future. Joseph Jaworski tells the remarkable story of his journey to an understanding of the deep issues of leadership. It is a personal journey that encourages and enlightens all of us wrestling with the profound changes required in public and institutional leadership, and in our individual lives, for the 21st century.

Hardcover, 228 pages, 6/96 • ISBN 1-881052-94-X
Item no. 5294X-212 $24.95

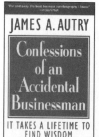

Confessions of an Accidental Businessman
It Takes a Lifetime to Find Wisdom

James A. Autry

IN *CONFESSIONS OF AN ACCIDENTAL BUSINESSMAN,* bestselling author James Autry blends candid and engaging autobiography with practical and realistic lessons in management and leadership. Reflecting on his thirty-two years in business, Autry shares a lifetime of hard-earned wisdom about the art of business leadership, as well as the art of living a balanced life.

Hardcover, 250 pages, 10/96 • ISBN 1-57675-003
Item no. 75003-212 $24.95

Available at your favorite bookstore, or call (800) 929-2929